In *Transformed*, Sus  ?n away from
a 'this is the way I   giving us real
hope that we coul   but by going
deeper into God'   through it to
bring real and last

                                              incy Guthrie
Bible teacher and author of the Seeing J.....   *Testament* series
                                           Nashville, Tennessee

With Susan Hunt's and Karen Hodge's book, the message of our
God's covenantal love is beautifully coordinated across generations of
women's leadership. With shared strength they show us how God's
grace renews minds and transforms lives to incarnate His creation
design and redemptive calling.

Bryan Chapell
Pastor
Grace Presbyterian Church
Peoria, Illinois

We all want to change and transform our lives. Too often, we look for
that transformation in all the wrong places. Susan and Karen's study
points us to the One who alone transforms us. Theologically rich,
Christ exalting, and based on our helper/life giver design, *Transformed*
will help you become what you behold.

Christina Fox
Author of *A Heart Set Free: A Journey to Hope Through the Psalms of Lament*.
Atlanta, Georgia

Reading *Transformed* is an opportunity to sit and learn from two gifted
and godly spiritual mothers. As Susan Hunt and Karen Hodge wisely
unpack the Scriptures, they purposefully point us to the One who can
transform us from life-takers to life-givers. With scripture readings,
insightful questions, and real-life stories this book is a helpful
encouragement to think biblically and live covenantally.

Melissa Kruger
Author of *The Envy of Eve* and *Walking with God in the Season of Motherhood*
Charlotte, North Carolina

Are you a Life-giver or a Life-taker? *Transformed* speaks directly into the
reality of all of us women, right here and right now, facing the challenge
between conformation and transformation. This outstanding work by
Karen Hodge and Susan Hunt clearly and uniquely displays powerful
insights of the effects of a life constantly and beautifully being shaped

into Christ's likeness. The truths in this book are real gems that will help equip you as you embrace and face the tension and opposition of the fight to become more and more like Jesus.

Daniele Flickinger
Passion City Church/FLOURISH Mentoring

Susan Hunt and Karen Hodge are kindred spirits who eagerly desire to see God's Word transform God's people from generation to generation. In *Transformed: Life-Taker to Life-Giver*, Susan and Karen provide solid biblical content in a way that will appeal to all generations. Through exploring key biblical texts; the accounts of Eve, Sarah and Mary; and the stories of contemporary believers, you will get a clearer picture of how a relationship with Christ transforms you to be an instrument of blessing in the hands of a sovereign and loving God.

Dr. Stephen Estock
Coordinator, PCA Discipleship Ministries

TRANSFORMED

LIFE-TAKER TO LIFE-GIVER

KAREN HODGE AND SUSAN HUNT

Susan is the wife of Gene Hunt, a retired PCA pastor, and they have 3 adult children and 12 grandchildren. She is the former PCA Coordinator for Women's Ministry. Susan is the author and co-author of several books for women's ministries including the newly released Titus 2 Tools as well as TRUE, a discipleship curriculum series on biblical womanhood for teen girls. She has also authored several books for children.

Karen is having the time of her life serving alongside her husband Chris, Senior Pastor at Naperville Presbyterian Church in Naperville, IL. Chris and Karen have two adult children Anna Grace Botka and Haddon Hodge that round out 'Team Hodge'. Karen serves as the current PCA Coordinator for Women's Ministry, where she seeks to connect women and churches to one another and to sound resources.

Copyright © Karen Hodge and Susan Hunt 2016

paperback ISBN: 978-1-78191-827-2
epub ISBN: 978-1-78191-897-5
mobi ISBN: 978-1-78191-898-2

10 9 8 7 6 5 4 3 2 1

Published in 2016
Reprinted in 2019
by
Christian Focus Publications Ltd,
Geanies House, Fearn,
Ross-shire, IV20 1TW, Scotland.
www.christianfocus.com

Cover design by Pete Barnsley, Creative Hoot
Printed and bound by Bell and Bain, Glasgow

MIX
Paper from responsible sources
FSC
www.fsc.org
FSC® C007785

CONTENTS

Oh, the depth of the riches and wisdom and knowledge of God! How unsearchable are his judgments and how inscrutable his ways!

"For who has known the mind of the Lord,
or who has been his counselor?"
"Or who has given a gift to him
that he might be repaid?"

For from him and through him and to him are all things. To him be glory forever. Amen.

I appeal to you therefore, brothers, by the mercies of God, to present your bodies as a living sacrifice, holy and acceptable to God, which is your spiritual worship. Do not be conformed to this world, but be transformed by the renewal of your mind, that by testing you may discern what is the will of God, what is good and acceptable and perfect.

(Rom. 11:33–12:2)

In memory of
Georgia Settle
who preceded Susan as Coordinator of Women's Ministry
for the Presbyterian Church in America

In honor of
Jane Patete
who followed Susan and preceded Karen as
Coordinator of Women's Ministry for the PCA

In partnership with
the company of transformed women who
went before us,
serve with us,
and will follow us

In gratitude for
Rev. Chris Hodge and Rev. Gene Hunt
Our Pastor/husbands who support, encourage, and love us

INTRODUCTION

OUR STORY

Susan: Almost thirty years ago I began serving as Coordinator of Women's Ministry for the Presbyterian Church in America. There were few resources for women's ministry so our first task was to develop biblical foundations for womanhood and for a women's ministry in the church. As we studied Scripture, we began to see the beauty of God's creation design of woman as a helper, and His redemptive calling to be life-givers. Then we began using these principles to disciple women. My first conversation with Karen knit my heart to hers. We soon recruited her to be one of our women's ministry trainers. It has been my joy to watch Karen grow as a pastor's wife, mom and women's ministry leader. Now, she is the Coordinator of Women's Ministry for the PCA. This spiritual daughter continues to wow me.

Karen: Almost 20 years ago Susan Hunt entered my life. I was a young bride, church planter's wife and a fairly overwhelmed mother of two. The rigors of church planting and the genesis of a women's ministry from the ground up found me desperate and scrambling for easy answers. When I called Susan and asked for the ten-step formula to start a stellar women's ministry, I quickly realized three things. First, there are no simple formulas but there are biblical principles. Second, the place to start is prayer. Third, I was not alone. As I humbly step into this calling of leading the denominational ministry to women that my spiritual mother fulfilled for so many years, I am incredibly grateful for her gracious, intentional investment in my life.

Susan: My ministry heartbeat is Titus 2 discipleship — women discipling women to glorify God by fulfilling our unique creation design (helper) and redemptive calling (life-giver). Not only does Karen share my passion for Titus 2, but she is taking it beyond anything I ever envisioned. Writing a book with this spiritual daughter is a rare privilege. I love that Karen is thirty years younger than me, and yet we speak "with one voice [to] glorify the God and Father of our Lord Jesus Christ" (Rom. 15:6).

Karen: Even though I had been heavily involved with women's ministry at the denominational level for many years, it was with a keen and urgent interest that I began asking Susan questions about how the principles of God's helper design and life-giver calling were developed. I am incredibly thankful for the solid theological foundation I stand upon in my role as coordinator. I see myself as both the beneficiary and the steward of these good gifts. My prayer is that women will not settle for just being informed about these principles but will ask God to transform them into women who live out the beauty of these truths in their lives, homes, workplaces, churches, and communities.

TRANSFORMED

Are you still trying to figure out who you want to be when you grow up? We face grown-up situations but deep down there is a little girl inside of us who wonders when she will be mature. Newsflash: *We are continually becoming what we will be, and we become what we behold.*

In the book of Romans, Paul climbs a great theological mountain. With every step, he builds his case about how to be made right with God. Then he reaches the summit and has a doxological moment.

Oh, the depth of the riches and wisdom and knowledge of God! How unsearchable are his judgments and how inscrutable his ways!

"For who has known the mind of the Lord,
or who has been his counselor?"
"Or who has given a gift to him
that he might be repaid?"

For from him and through him and to him are all things. To him be glory forever. Amen.

(Rom. 11:33-36)

Paul's questions help us behold the greatness of God and our inability to add anything to who He is. We are products of our theology and our doxology. What we believe about God, and what we esteem and elevate as praiseworthy, will profoundly shape our lives. Our theology and doxology are inseparably connected. Worship is the overflow of the revelation of God in Scripture, so after beholding the greatness and the grace of God Paul makes his appeal to us.

I appeal to you therefore, brothers, by the mercies of God, to present your bodies as a living sacrifice, holy and acceptable to God, which is your spiritual worship. Do not be conformed to this world, but be transformed by the renewal of your mind, that by testing you may discern what is the will of God, what is good and acceptable and perfect (Rom. 12:1-2). Sound theology and doxology compel us to surrender. Presenting our bodies as living sacrifices entails hands, ears, mouths, minds, spleens and everything else. In the Old Testament, there were two basic kinds of sacrifices. In the sin offering an unblemished animal was slain for the atonement of sins, yet the remains of the animal could be used to feed the priest's family. Paul refers to the burnt offering when an unblemished animal was burned on the altar until it was totally consumed; nothing was used for other purposes. *Living* means alive and active. *Sacrifice* means death. How can we be a *living killing*? Paul explains: "I have been crucified with Christ. It is no longer I who live, but Christ who lives in me. And the life I now live in the flesh I live by faith in the Son of God, who loved me and gave himself for me" (Gal. 2:20).

Being a *living killing* is our spiritual worship. In light of the mercies of God, it is the logical and rational thing to do, but it is not natural, so Paul urges us not to "be conformed to this world."

Conformation is the opposite of transformation in this passage. Conformity happens when the continual pressures of the world, the flesh and the devil mold or morph us into their likeness. The word *conformed* finds its roots in the word for masquerade. We feel guilty and hypocritical when we try to play the part of the perfect friend, wife, mother or daughter, but we don't have to pretend. Paul holds before us the exhilarating idea of *transformation*.

Transformation is the process whereby the Holy Spirit effects such a radical, revolutionary change in our hearts that it is revealed in our affections, ambitions, actions and attitudes. It is rooted in the same word for metamorphosis — a profound difference between the beginning and ending. The most familiar example of metamorphosis is the caterpillar changing into a butterfly. The caterpillar forms a chrysalis and does not become a butterfly by being smart enough or strong enough to effect the change. It is only when the caterpillar is still that transformation occurs. And when the process is complete there is absolutely nothing in the splendor of the butterfly that resembles the former likeness of the caterpillar. The power of a greater force, outside itself, brings about the glorious difference.

In this passage, the verb *transformed* is in the present tense, which means it is ongoing. It is also in the passive voice which literally means *let yourself be* transformed, *yield* to transformation, and you will begin to discern God's will. We grow up as the Holy Spirit renews our minds and realigns our hearts so that our thinking and living are no longer make-believe – we are believable. We become what we were created and redeemed to be.

Now the Lord is the Spirit, and where the Spirit of the Lord is, there is freedom. And we all, with unveiled face, beholding the glory of the Lord, are being transformed into the same image from one degree of glory to another. For this comes from the Lord who is the Spirit. (2 Cor. 3:17-18)

We become what we behold.

Life-Giver

When the first man and woman sinned against God, they deserved the death sentence but received the gospel promise of Life through a Redeemer, and grace upon grace this Life would come through woman (Gen. 3:15). In response, Adam gave his wife a new name that sounds like the Hebrew word for life-giver — Eve (Gen. 3:20).

The gospel brought a radical reversal of what our first parents expected and deserved (death), and how they had behaved (disobedience to God; disloyalty to one another). This reversal is celebrated by the name Adam gave her.

When we are saved, our *potential* changes from life-taker to life-giver because our *status* has changed: "Whoever has the Son has life; whoever does not have the Son of God does not have life" (1 John 5:12).

Birthing a child — *a life* — is a beautiful illustration of our redemptive calling to be life-givers, but the ultimate demonstration is when the Life of Christ fills us and spills out onto our circumstances and relationships. Our redemptive calling transcends age, life-season, marital status, time and place in history. It is big. *Really big.* It is a calling to live boldly and Biblically. It is a life-long adventure of "beholding the glory of the Lord [and] being transformed into the same image from one degree of glory to another ... " (2 Cor. 3:18).

THIS BOOK

This book is a combination of Bible study (Thinking Biblically) and devotional readings (Living Covenantally).

Objective of Thinking Biblically

- For your mind to be renewed as you develop Bible study skills that help you discover Jesus in all of Scripture by seeing the unified message of redemption that unfolds throughout the Bible.

Objective of Living Covenantally

- To challenge you to apply the message of grace so that your life is transformed by God's grace.

These Bible studies and devotions are designed to be easily accessible and in short morsels of truth that you can digest on the go.

We will begin with Peter's reference to "holy women who hoped in God" (1 Pet. 3:1-7) and then look at the stories of three such women. Peter's letter gives the larger context to understand these stories.

- Eve, the mother of all the living, will teach us about our creation design (helper), the Promise of Life, and our redemptive calling to be life-givers.

- Sarah, the mother of those who hope in the Promise, will take us deeper into "the riches and wisdom and knowledge of God" (Rom. 11:33) that renew our minds so we know and do His will.

- Mary, the mother of Jesus, will teach us that the baby she birthed at the dawn of the New Testament is the Promised One, the Giver of Life, who transforms us into life-givers.

Eve, Sarah and Mary will show us the process of God's grace renewing their minds and transforming their lives so they incarnate His creation design and redemptive calling.

THE NEED

The cultural confusion and chaos about gender is obvious, but that is not the reason for this book. Admittedly, our cultural environment intensifies the need for gender-specific discipleship, but regardless of our time and place in history, God created us male and female and His people need to know His design and plan. Whatever our gender, age, marital status, circumstances or location on the globe, our purpose is to glorify God. To fulfill this glorious purpose, we must be transformed in every area of life, including our sexuality, by God's Word and not conformed to the world's standards.

Our Prayer

Our prayer is that this book will be a tool to disciple you to think biblically and live covenantally, but we understand that we can only disciple you from a distance. We do not live life with you. We hope you will use this book as a group study with women who will love you, and whom you can love, "like a nursing mother taking care of her own children" and with whom you can "share ... not only the gospel of God but also [your] own selves" (1 Thess. 2:7-8). Covenant community life, characterized by nurturing, gospel-centered relationships, provides a safe place for the Lord to transform you from life-taker to life-giver and a good place to celebrate His transforming grace in others.

A Leader's Guide for this book
and resources for women's ministry in the church
are available from the Presbyterian Church in America
Committee on Discipleship

http://www.cepbookstore.com/

1-800-283-1357

ONE

The Glory Story

1 Peter 1 and 3

ANDREA'S STORY

Dr. Andrea Johnson is a medical oncologist specializing in breast cancer. She lives in Charlotte, North Carolina.

I grew up in a Christian home, married a godly man and we settled into a church community. Our family grew to five kids, including two adopted daughters. I am a physician with many demands. Life is fast and full.

Despite years of sound Bible teaching, the doctrine of biblical womanhood was never much the focus. I heard teaching for women regarding marriage, friendships, a gentle and quiet spirit, all great topics, but I either missed or was not taught the life-altering theology of why God made woman distinct from man. I found myself in my forties and hearing for the first time a rich biblical perspective of womanhood. New terms such as "a woman's helper design" and "life-giving calling" started to settle into my thoughts.

I'm all about the helper and life-giver at work, after all, I'm a physician — and I have surrounded myself with a nurse, secretary and nanny to help me be a better helper and life-giver to others. This subtly developed into a self-centered approach to life where all *my* helpers were in place to help *me*. As you can imagine, this set my marriage and family life off course.

My focal point was off center and I became disappointed with unmet expectations from all these extenders, including my own husband at times.

Thankfully we are in a church where I now receive clear teaching about God's creation design and redemptive calling for women. These truths are like water to a thirsty soul. There are women who model these truths to me and disciple me to apply them to my life. They have redirected me to a healthier balance in my marriage and other relationships by encouraging me to ask myself basic questions.

- Am I being a helper or a hinderer?

- Am I being a life-giver or a life-taker?

- Is God's glory my purpose rather than my own agenda and convenience?

Life is still fast and full, but I'm excited to model and teach the truth of womanhood to my daughters. They are growing up in a crazy culture that is increasingly androgynous. I want them to be grounded in a biblical perspective of womanhood.

THINKING BIBLICALLY

The imperatives (what we are to do) are always a consequence of the indicatives (who we are by God's gracious provision); what we do is never a cause of who we are with respect to our eternal status in God's kingdom and family. We obey as a result of being God's beloved, not to cause God to love us. His grace toward us precedes, enables, and motivates our efforts toward holiness.[1]

Dr. Bryan Chapell

1 Peter 1

¹Peter, an apostle of Jesus Christ, To those who are elect exiles of the dispersion in Pontus, Galatia, Cappadocia, Asia, and Bithynia,

²according to the foreknowledge of God the Father, in the sanctification of the Spirit, for obedience to Jesus Christ and for sprinkling with his blood: May grace and peace be multiplied to you.

³Blessed be the God and Father of our Lord Jesus Christ! According to his great mercy, he has caused us to be born again to a living hope through the resurrection of Jesus Christ from the dead,

⁴to an inheritance that is imperishable, undefiled, and unfading, kept in heaven for you,

⁵who by God's power are being guarded through faith for a salvation ready to be revealed in the last time.

- Underline words that describe our status because of God's provision.
- Which persons of the Trinity are mentioned?
- Circle the word that describes hope.
- What is the basis of this hope?
- How does Peter describe a Christian's inheritance?

In his letter to Christians who were scattered throughout what is now Turkey, Peter's primary purpose was to answer an always relevant question: How do Christians face persecution and hardship?

Hardship and holiness: these are the twin themes of Peter's first epistle, written to a church composed of Gentile converts from licentious hedonism on the one hand and Jewish converts with Old Testament traditions on the other hand. Together they experienced an alien and exile status in a hostile world ... Peter's words on holiness and hardship are inextricably connected. Because of the way the Spirit conforms us to the image of Christ, Peter not only sees holiness as necessary for enduring hardship; he sees hardship as a way the Spirit makes us holy.[2]

Peter's answer to the question of how Christians face hardships is also an essential element of transformation: trust and obey. "Therefore let those who suffer according to God's will entrust their souls to a faithful Creator [trust] while doing good [obey]" (1 Pet. 4:19). Peter writes to God's elect people to encourage them to hold fast to hope.

Hope is not simply a feeling or desire. *I hope it won't rain tomorrow* is based on circumstances. Peter calls us to a living hope that is rooted in a relationship with a living Savior. It is the sure hope of an inheritance that will never perish, be defiled, or fade because it is guarded by God.

6In this you rejoice, though now for a little while, if necessary, you have been grieved by various trials,

7so that the tested genuineness of your faith—more precious than gold that perishes though it is tested by fire—may be found to result in praise and glory and honor at the revelation of Jesus Christ.

- What is the "this" that we are to rejoice in?
- How are hardships and hope connected?

Hope and hardships are companions on this pilgrimage. We rejoice in our hope even as we grieve over our hardships. But we do "not grieve as others do who have no hope" (1 Thess. 4:13).

13Therefore, preparing your minds for action, and being sober-minded, set your hope fully on the grace that will be brought to you at the revelation of Jesus Christ.

14As obedient children, do not be conformed to the passions of your former ignorance,

15but as he who called you is holy, you also be holy in all your conduct,

16since it is written, "You shall be holy, for I am holy."

- What are the imperatives?
- How does he describe our status in verse 14?
- What are your thoughts about being God's child?
- Circle the word holy.

Now holiness joins the journey. Holiness is necessary to endure hardships and the Spirit uses hardships to make us holy. Our positional holiness is the result of God's grace. Practical holiness comes as we prepare our minds, set our hope, and obey our Father rather than yield to the gravitational pull to be conformed to the past.

[17] And if you call on him as Father who judges impartially according to each one's deeds, conduct yourselves with fear throughout the time of your exile,

[18] knowing that you were ransomed from the futile ways inherited from your forefathers, not with perishable things such as silver or gold,

[19] but with the precious blood of Christ, like that of a lamb without blemish or spot.

[20] He was foreknown before the foundation of the world but was made manifest in the last times for the sake of you

[21] who through him are believers in God, who raised him from the dead and gave him glory, so that your faith and hope are in God.

- How are we to live as exiles?
- Why are we to live this way?
- Underline what the passage says about God.

Our reference point for holiness is the Triune God. Despite our circumstances, Peter challenges us to "conduct ourselves with fear"— to live in awe of God's holiness, respect His authority, and reverently worship Him in Spirit and in truth. Gratitude that we are ransomed exiles continually leads us, as it did Peter, to doxological moments (vv. 19-21) and covenantal living (v. 22).

22 Having purified your souls by your obedience to the truth for a sincere brotherly love, love one another earnestly from a pure heart,

23 since you have been born again, not of perishable seed but of imperishable, through the living and abiding word of God;

24 for "All flesh is like grass and all its glory like the flower of grass. The grass withers, and the flower falls,

25 but the word of the Lord remains forever." And this word is the good news that was preached to you.

- What is the imperative?
- What is the power to obey the imperative?

As we trust and obey God's Word, our souls are purified and we begin to love our brothers and sisters. If you want to know if God is transforming you, look at your relationships, especially those with difficult people. We are like grass that blooms and passes away, *but* the gospel seed planted in our hearts never dies. It grows and produces gospel fruit. So what do holy, hopeful women invest their lives in? The only two things that last forever; the Word of God and the souls of men.

LIVING COVENANTALLY

I believe in ... the communion of the saints.

The Apostles' Creed

Glory for Suffering Women: 1 Peter 3:1-7

*Oh, the depth of the riches and wisdom and knowledge of God ...
To him be glory forever ... Do not be conformed to this world, but
be transformed by the renewal of your mind.* (Rom. 11:33–12:2)

Peter has been called the apostle of hope. In chapter 3, he
specifically addresses the women. These women are exiles. Fear
of persecution is their daily reality. Peter writes:

*Likewise, wives, be subject to your own husbands, so that even if
some do not obey the word, they may be won without a word by
the conduct of their wives, when they see your respectful and pure
conduct. Do not let your adorning be external, the braiding of hair,
the putting on of gold jewelry, or the clothing you wear but let your
adorning be the hidden person of the heart with the imperishable
beauty of a gentle and quiet spirit, which in God's sight is very
precious. For this is how the holy women who hoped in God used to
adorn themselves, by submitting to their husbands, as Sarah obeyed
Abraham, calling him lord. And you are her children, if you do good
and do not fear anything that is frightening. Likewise, husbands,
live with your wives in an understanding way, showing honor to the
woman as the weaker vessel, since they are heirs with you of the
grace of life, so that your prayers may not be hindered.* (1 Pet. 3:1-7)

Do you want to ask Peter, "Is this the best you've got for suffering
women? Telling them to submit when they are trying to survive
— really? Is warning them about external clothing relevant? And
what does the example of ancient women have to do with their
very current fears about living in a strange land?" On first-read,
this seems to be an insensitive, behavioral to-do list.

That's the problem with a first-read. Unless we see the
context, we miss the glory.

If we lift any portion of Scripture out of context we usually
walk away with a diminished and distorted understanding.
Pastor Peter's first word to the women, *likewise*, puts his
instructions in the context of everything he has said. Then
he gives three electrifying descriptions of the women he uses
as examples. Peter points suffering women to Old Testament
spiritual mothers who were holy, hopeful, heirs of the grace of
life. This practical pastor emphasizes that some discipleship is to
be gender-specific, just as Paul instructed Titus:

But as for you, teach what accords with sound doctrine ... Older women likewise are to be reverent in behavior, not slanderers or slaves to much wine. They are to teach what is good, and so train the young women to love their husbands and children, to be self-controlled, pure, working at home, kind, and submissive to their own husbands, that the word of God may not be reviled. (Titus 2:3-5)

Titus 2 discipleship aims for transformed lives that honor God's Word. Scattered, suffering women need spiritual mothers to tell them about the "depth of the riches and wisdom and knowledge of God!" and to show them how this glorious gospel empowers them to "not be conformed to this world, but be transformed by the renewal of your mind" (Rom. 11:33; 12:1). Women need other women to encourage and equip them to trust and obey, even in hard places and relationships.

Points to Ponder

Gospel imperatives (things we are commanded to do) are always grounded in gospel indicatives (our status in Christ).

Peter celebrates our status when he refers to us as heirs of the grace of life (1 Pet. 3:7).

If you trust Christ for your salvation, you are an heir of the grace of life — think about that.

Transformed by Prayer

My heart is steadfast, O God!

I will sing and make melody with all my being! ...

I will give thanks to you, O LORD, among the peoples;

I will sing praises to you among the nations.

For your steadfast love is great above the heavens;

your faithfulness reaches to the clouds.

Be exalted, O God, above the heavens!

Let your glory be over all the earth!

(Ps. 108:1-5)

Scope of the Whole: 1 Peter 3:1-7

Q. 1. What is the chief end of man?

A. Man's chief end is to glorify God, and to enjoy him forever.[3]

The Westminster Shorter Catechism

The women who first heard Peter's instructions heard them in the context of everything he had already said. His reference to Old Testament women and quotes also pointed them to the overarching scope of the redemption story.

The Bible is God's riveting revelation of Himself to His people. It is the sweeping story of the redemption planned in eternity past, accomplished in time, and applied to individuals by the Triune God. *The Westminster Larger Catechism* proclaims, "The scriptures manifest themselves to be the word of God, by their majesty and purity; by the consent of all the parts, and the scope of the whole, which is to give all glory to God ... "[4]

Lock the "consent and scope" principle into your mind and heart. Every part of Scripture agrees with every other part because there is a "scope of the whole" which is the Glorious Gospel Story. This story not only spans centuries, it stretches from eternity past into eternity future. Unless we understand the "scope" (the meta-narrative) of Scripture our understanding of each part will be diminished. No story, person, event or instruction stands alone. There is a perfect unity that is breathtaking because, according to Jesus, it all tells His Story: "And beginning with Moses and all the Prophets, he interpreted to them in all the Scriptures the things concerning himself" (Luke 24:27).

We trace the flow of the redemption story through the lives of men and women until we reach the high point in history when our Savior Jesus came in grace and lived among us. The story did not end with His victorious resurrection and ascension. The consummate climax will be when King Jesus comes back in glory. But between His two comings, where is glory? It would be scandalous to say it if He had not said it:

The glory that you have given me I have given to them [that would be you and me!], that they may be one even as we are one, I in them and you in me, that they may become perfectly one, so that the world may know that you sent me and loved them even as you loved me. (John 17:22-23)

Eve, Sarah and Mary, three holy women who hoped in God, will help us see the scope of the whole, and that not only does every part of Scripture agree, but every part of their lives agrees with every other part to give all glory to God. These spiritual mothers will show us that no matter how chaotic life seems at eye level, nothing is random — God uses everything to lovingly transform us into the likeness of Jesus.

These mothers in the faith point us to Jesus. They show us the journey from gloom to glory, from hopeless to hopeful, from life-taker to life-giver. They don't sugar-coat it. It is a slow, hard, painful, lonely, scary, beautifully redemptive journey through the wilderness. Their ragged, sometimes racy, lives show that the persevering grace of God is unstoppable. Glory wins because the Father loves us even as He loves Jesus. He gives us His glory so we can reflect His glory even in hard places.

*P*oints to *P*onder

Why does Jesus give us His glory?

What are your thoughts about nothing in your life being random?

How have holy, hopeful women encouraged you to trust and obey God's Word?

How are you encouraging others?

Transformed by Prayer

Let my cry come before you, O LORD;

give me understanding according to your word!

Let my plea come before you;

deliver me according to your word.

My lips will pour forth praise,

for you teach me your statutes.

My tongue will sing of your word,

for all your commandments are right.

(Ps. 119:169-172)

Holy, Hopeful, Exiles: 1 Peter 1:1-3

Lift up your heads, O gates!

And lift them up, O ancient doors, that the King of glory may come in.

Who is this King of glory? The Lord of hosts, he is the King of glory!

(Ps. 24:9-10)

Like the recipients of Peter's letter, we increasingly feel like strangers living among people who neither understand nor support our way of life. Peter does not waste time treating these exiles as victims. With an incredible economy of words, he points them (and us) to three doctrines that give security and stability in the midst of uncertainty and unbelief.

First, he identifies them as "elect exiles" (1 Pet. 1:1). The doctrine of election plunges us into the magnificent mystery of God's absolute sovereignty over all things, including our salvation and transformation. Dr. John MacArthur writes, "Election is such a powerful truth that when Christians understand it, the practical ramifications of election will transform the way they live their daily lives."[5]

Second, Peter connects our election to the work of the Trinity in accomplishing our salvation.

"... according to the foreknowledge of God the Father" (v. 2) does not simply mean that God looked into the future and *predicted* what would happen; He *planned* it. Peter's reference to God as Father is deliberate. They are suffering. They need to remember God as a tender Father who loves them and as the King of Glory who sovereignly chose them.

"In the sanctification of the Spirit" (v. 2) means that our election is made effectual by the Holy Spirit.

"For obedience to Jesus Christ and for sprinkling with his blood" (v. 2) brilliantly fuses our history and calling. The sprinkling imagery reaches back to the Old Testament when blood was used:

1. To confirm the covenant God made with His people (Exod. 24:3-8);

36

2. As an offering to atone for sin, pointing to the substitutionary sacrifice of Jesus for our sin (Lev. 16:15-16; Heb. 9:11-14);

3. To consecrate, or set apart, for service (Exod. 29:21; Heb. 10:19-25).

This Trinitarian shape of the gospel assures us that salvation and sanctification are not dependent on us. The Spirit sanctifies those the Father chose and the Son died for, so they can trust and obey.

Peter does not ignore our suffering, but he speaks into it something that will transform our hardship into our holiness: "May grace and peace be multiplied to you" (v. 2).

Peter's wonderment is palpable as he reminds them of the hinge of their hope – the resurrection.

> ... According to his great mercy, he has caused us to be born again to a living hope through the resurrection of Jesus Christ from the dead. (1 Pet. 2:3)

The doctrine of the resurrection is the security of our new birth, the basis for our hope, the power for our holiness, and the assurance of our inheritance.

There are probably no doctrines that incentivize and energize God's suffering children to trust and obey, more than His sovereign election, His Trinitarian being, and His resurrection from the dead. Peter's intensity in pointing us to the gospel is understandable - he had forgotten the gospel and denied Jesus, but the Risen Christ said to him, "Feed my sheep" (John 21:17).

Points to Ponder

In 1 Peter chapter 3 Peter uses three words to describe the women he wants us to learn from — holy, hopeful, heirs.

Was this the first time his readers heard these words? (See 1 Peter chapter 1.)

Who are women you know that you would describe as holy and hopeful? Tell them.

Transformed by Prayer

To you, O LORD, I lift up my soul.

O my God, in you I trust ...

Make me to know your ways, O LORD;

teach me your paths.

Lead me in your truth and teach me,

for you are the God of my salvation;

for you I wait all the day long.

Remember your mercy, O LORD, and your steadfast love,

for they have been from of old.

(Ps. 25:1-6)

Holy, Hopeful, Heirs of the Covenant: 1 Peter 1

The friendship of the LORD is for those who fear him, and he makes known to them his covenant.

(Ps. 25:14)

The holy women Peter refers to did not simply hope for a change in their circumstances; they hoped in God. These "heirs according to promise" (Gal. 3:29) hoped in God's covenant promise that stretches from Genesis to Revelation: I will be your God, you will be my people, I will live among you.

How can this be? Is there really a way that sinful rebels can live in a relationship with Sovereign Love? Is there a way that I can be His? Isn't the space between us too big? Isn't He too far away?

> The distance between God and the creature is so great, that although reasonable creatures do owe obedience unto Him as their Creator, yet they could never have any fruition of Him as their blessedness and reward, but by some voluntary condescension on God's part, which he hath been pleased to express by way of covenant.[6]

It took a covenant to bring Glory near.

Covenant is a compelling idea. Covenant is the storyline of the Glory Story, a story that began before the beginning of time when God chose us in Christ to be His own (Eph. 1:4), that exploded into time and space when God created us in His image (Gen. 1), was scandalously lost when our first parents rebelled (Gen. 3:1-7), was graciously restored when God promised a Redeemer (Gen. 3:15), was gloriously fulfilled when the Word became flesh (John 1:14), and will reach its spectacular consummation when we hear " ... a loud voice from the throne saying, 'Behold, the dwelling place of God is with man. He will dwell with them, and they will be his people, and God himself will be with them as their God'" (Rev. 21:3).

The covenant is Trinitarian. In the pre-creation covenant of redemption the Father chose a people, the Son redeemed them by His blood, and the Holy Spirit applies what the Father purposed and the Son accomplished. Peter's starting point in his letter to suffering Christians is the Trinitarian shape of the gospel (1 Pet. 1:1-2).

The covenant is nurturing. I think this is why, as a woman, my heart is drawn to this tender "condescension on God's part" to adopt us as His children, nurture us, and prepare a home where we can live with Him forever. Peter reminds people who had probably lost their earthly inheritance, of the eternal inheritance that is imperishable.

The covenant is relational. The God of all glory enters into a relationship with His chosen ones. He adopts us into His family on the basis of the finished work of Christ. Peter calls us to live covenantally by loving one another, even in hard places (1 Pet. 1:22-23). Covenant life involves sharing the gospel and our lives because we love each other.

> But we were gentle among you, like a nursing mother taking care of her own children.
>
> So, being affectionately desirous of you, we were ready to share with you not only the gospel of God but also our own selves, because you had become very dear to us. (1 Thess. 2:7-8)

When holy, hopeful women live covenantally by sharing the gospel and their lives, they disciple other women to be holy and hopeful.

Points to Ponder

What is one thing about God's covenant of grace that you love?

What difference does it make to hear the gospel from someone who first shares her life with you?

How are you sharing the gospel and your life with others?

Transformed by Prayer

In you, O LORD, do I take refuge;

let me never be put to shame;

in your righteousness deliver me!

Incline your ear to me;

rescue me speedily!

Be a rock of refuge for me,

a strong fortress to save me!

For you are my rock and my fortress;

and for your name's sake you lead me and guide me ...

Oh, how abundant is your goodness,

which you have stored up for those who fear you

and worked for those who take refuge in you ...

(Ps. 31:1-3, 19).

Bifurcated Women: Titus 2

Blessed are those who keep his testimonies,
who seek him with their whole heart.

(Ps. 119:2)

I (Karen) consider the bifurcation of faith and life to be the greatest threat to my own heart and the hearts of women I know. Redeemed women need to know that faith is not just a part of life; it is our whole life.

Bifurcation is not a word that readily rolls off the tongue around the dinner table. Its Latin root is from "bi", two pronged, and "fork", to divide. It is the proverbial fork in the road — the place where faith and life are integrated or separated. It is the place of disconnect between belief and behavior. It is the point of transformation or conformation. It is what some call "living a life of practical atheism" — living as though God does not exist even when you intellectually assent that He does.

This division in my own heart became glaringly apparent when my husband was called to plant a church in South Florida, a secular and de-churched area. I grew up in a different spiritual climate filled with discipleship relationships and opportunities. My husband believes that an evangelistic-focused women's ministry is integral in establishing a healthy church. I share his conviction. Very quickly the Lord brought to our church women who were hungry for answers, but I soon realized they wanted and needed more than my formulaic answers. They wanted authenticity. The gap between what I know, and how to show it in a transparent manner, challenged me towards a new level of vulnerability. They needed to see what Paul explained to Titus when he wrote to instruct him how to have a healthy church.

> *But as for you, teach what accords with sound doctrine ... Older women likewise are to be reverent in behavior, not slanderers or slaves to much wine. They are to teach what is good, and so train the young women ... that the word of God may not be reviled.*
> (Titus 2:1-5)

Titus was the pastor of the church in Crete. The culture of Crete and the culture of the western hemisphere are not dissimilar.

Like Titus, we are surrounded by the false and toxic doctrines of this world. In this environment, Paul told Titus to teach sound doctrine and to equip his congregation for life-on-life discipleship, including older women training younger women.

The root of the word "sound" is from the word hygienic. Sound doctrine is healthy. It makes sick people well. The Greek word "train" means to show, model or demonstrate. As Paul explains, "Show yourself in all respects to be a model of good works ... so that in everything they may adorn the doctrine of God our Savior" (Titus 2:7-10). Peter, too, exhorts us to adorn our hearts with "the imperishable beauty of a gentle and quiet spirit" (1 Pet. 3:3-5). To adorn something is to put it on display. When sound doctrine flows out into sound living, toxic relationships become whole. Unhealthy churches become strong and vigorous. And God's Word is not reviled.

Back to Florida. My husband preaches sound doctrine. The women needed me to put the gospel on display. God tenderly showed me the shallowness of being merely informed. He showed me that His plan for us is infinitely more radical than knowing information. His plan is total transformation from the inside out. It has been, and continues to be, a glorious, messy metamorphosis.

I am still tempted to default to simplistic solutions when life and ministry are hard. The Spirit uses many friends who model preaching the gospel to their own heart, and who gently preach it to my heart as well. The mutuality of biblical community is a profound tool in my transformation.

A life that is integrated and whole, with no division between faith and life, puts Jesus on display.

Points to Ponder

Are there areas of your life where your behavior is disconnected from your belief?

Why do you think we need someone to show us what a gospel-centered life looks like?

Who are the people who teach you sound doctrine? Thank them.

Who are some people you know who put the gospel on display? Thank them.

Transformed by Prayer

Teach me your way, O LORD,

that I may walk in your truth;

unite my heart to fear your name.

I give thanks to you, O LORD my God, with my whole heart,

and I will glorify your name forever.

For great is your steadfast love toward me;

you have delivered my soul from the depths of Sheol.

(Ps. 86:11-13).

Two

Transformed

1 Peter 2–3

LAUREN'S STORY

Lauren duBois, from Chicago, Illinois, is a partner in an executive search firm.

I made bad choices in college. Then I dropped out, got married, and had two daughters. It was an abusive marriage and after eight years we divorced. My ex-husband defaulted on child support and my parents would not help me. Needing to support myself and my children, I worked hard and had professional success in a male-dominated sales field. Alone with small children and no help, I felt unworthy of God's love and began to doubt His existence.

Another marriage, another child, another divorce, again no child support. But, this time I paid alimony. I became an angry woman with little respect for men. I joined National Organization of Women and marched in support of abortion rights. I was independent. I needed and trusted no one but myself. *A woman needs a man like a fish needs a bicycle* was my anthem.

Then 9/11 happened. As the World Trade Center fell, so did my world. In that chaos, I turned to God and He became my hope. I met and married a kind man. But at heart, I was still an angry feminist.

In 2008, several friends and I attended the first True Woman conference. As Mary Kassian explained the history of the women's movement and the social damage it had done, I found myself nodding in total agreement. As Susan Hunt talked about biblical womanhood, my eyes were opened to the ways I had been a life-taker. I embraced the truth of my helper design and redemptive calling to be a life-giver.

I once thought my past was unredeemable, but the power of the gospel transformed this life-taker into a woman who leads Bible studies for women in my church.

Many women share my story and are living in hopelessness. I pray there will be many life-givers who tell them the creation and redemption story and who show them the transforming love of Jesus.

THINKING BIBLICALLY

The infallible rule of interpretation of Scripture is the Scripture itself: and therefore, when there is a question about the true and full sense of any Scripture (which is not manifold, but one), it must be searched and known by other places that speak more clearly.[1]

Westminster Confession of Faith

1 Peter 2

¹*So put away all malice and all deceit and hypocrisy and envy and all slander.*

²*Like newborn infants, long for the pure spiritual milk, that by it you may grow up to salvation –*

³*if indeed you have tasted that the Lord is good.*

- What does the first word, So, refer back to?
- What is the imperative?
- What transforms our appetites?

Peter says, "The word of the Lord remains forever" (1 Pet. 1:25) so he encourages spiritual growth by encouraging us to examine our appetites. He mentions life-taking actions and attitudes that are the overflow of spiritually malnourished people. What we feed upon matters. Tasting the goodness of the Lord whets our appetites for more truth so Peter challenges us to let our appetites be transformed by feasting on God's Word.

⁴*As you come to him, a living stone rejected by men but in the sight of God chosen and precious,*

⁵*you yourselves like living stones are being built up as a spiritual house, to be a holy priesthood, to offer spiritual sacrifices acceptable to God through Jesus Christ.*

⁶*For it stands in Scripture: "Behold, I am laying in Zion a stone, a cornerstone chosen and precious, and whoever believes in him will not be put to shame."*

⁷*So the honor is for you who believe, but for those who do not believe, "The stone that the builders rejected has become the cornerstone,"*

⁸*and "A stone of stumbling, and a rock of offense." They stumble because they disobey the word, as they were destined to do.*

⁹*But you are a chosen race, a royal priesthood, a holy nation, a people for his own possession, that you may proclaim the excellencies of him who called you out of darkness into his marvelous light.*

[10]Once you were not a people, but now you are God's people; once you had not received mercy, but now you have received mercy.

- What do you learn about your identity in Christ?
- What do you learn about your connection to other believers?
- Underline the reason some stumble.
- How does Peter contrast our before-and-after status in verse 10?
- Identify some edges of your heart that need to be smoothed away in order for you to fit together with those around you.

Deep within every heart is the desire to belong. Our identity in Christ gives us people and place. Life together in the body of Christ, on the smallest scale or in the grandest fashion, allows us to enter one of God's ordained catalysts for our transformation. The Chief Cornerstone chooses, enlivens and reshapes us so we fit together to become a spiritual structure to house His presence. As we delight in the unity and diversity of fellow sojourners, we begin to get a glimpse of God's intended purpose found in the original community – the Triune God. Biblical community is a sanctifying foretaste of heaven as God transforms life-less stones into life-giving saints.

[11]Beloved, I urge you as sojourners and exiles to abstain from the passions of the flesh, which wage war against your soul.

[12]Keep your conduct among the Gentiles honorable, so that when they speak against you as evildoers, they may see your good deeds and glorify God on the day of visitation.

[13]Be subject for the Lord's sake to every human institution, whether it be to the emperor as supreme,

[14]or to governors as sent by him to punish those who do evil and to praise those who do good.

[15]For this is the will of God, that by doing good you should put to silence the ignorance of foolish people.

16Live as people who are free, not using your freedom as a cover-up for evil, but living as servants of God.

17Honor everyone. Love the brotherhood. Fear God. Honor the emperor.

18Servants, be subject to your masters with all respect, not only to the good and gentle but also to the unjust.

19For this is a gracious thing, when, mindful of God, one endures sorrows while suffering unjustly.

20For what credit is it if, when you sin and are beaten for it, you endure? But if when you do good and suffer for it you endure, this is a gracious thing in the sight of God.

- Underline the imperatives.
- Read the passage again and put brackets around the reasons given for the imperatives.
- Circle the words subject and servants.
- Describe the war within your heart between resisting and relinquishing.
- What has to die in order for us to submit?

There is a war going on and the frontline is a battle for our hearts. The inclination of our heart is to resist and rebel rather than submit. Submission is never natural. It is supernatural. It is never passive and must be intentional.

Peter unpacks the imperatives of our transformed inclinations. The rubber hits the road in the context of community. He moves from the most distant (the emperor) to the most intimate (husbands in 3:1) of relationships. To be subject is to submit, yield, relinquish or surrender. The postures of worship and surrender are identical, they are openhanded. Living openhandedly may seem frightening, but ultimately it is freeing. Christ is our reference point for submission. He opened His hands, letting go of heaven and submitting to crucifixion in our place. We are never more like Christ than when we submit.

²¹*For to this you have been called, because Christ also suffered for you, leaving you an example, so that you might follow in his steps.*

²²*He committed no sin, neither was deceit found in his mouth.*

²³*When he was reviled, he did not revile in return; when he suffered, he did not threaten, but continued entrusting himself to him who judges justly.*

²⁴*He himself bore our sins in his body on the tree, that we might die to sin and live to righteousness. By his wounds you have been healed.*

²⁵*For you were straying like sheep, but have now returned to the Shepherd and Overseer of your souls.*

- What do you learn about Jesus in these verses?

As we increasingly entrust ourselves to Him who judges justly, the Spirit transforms our identities, appetites and inclinations so that we begin to look more and more like Christ.

LIVING COVENANTALLY

The communion of saints is the living fellowship of all true believers who are united in love by their union with Christ and have spiritual communion with one another as they share in corporate worship, spiritual gifts, Christian graces, material goods, and mutual edification.[2]

Philip Graham Ryken

Redeemed Reality: 1 Peter 2:1-10

Oh, taste and see that the Lord is good!
Blessed is the man who takes refuge in him!

(Ps. 34:8)

Peter piles up gospel realities in chapter one and then shifts to gospel imperatives: "So put away all malice and all deceit and hypocrisy and envy and all slander" (1 Pet. 2:1).

My reality – I can't do this. I can pretend. I can make you think I have. But ugly stuff slinks in my heart. Pastor Peter is so pastoral. He acknowledges our inability to be good by pointing us again to the One who is good: "Like newborn infants, long for the pure spiritual milk, that by it you may grow up to salvation – if indeed you have tasted that the Lord is good" (1 Pet. 2:2-3).

I can't change my heart but I can increase my appetite for what is good. I can develop the holy habit of reading my Bible. The more I taste His goodness, the more bitter sin tastes, and the more my affections, ambitions, attitudes, and actions are shaped by His Word. I begin to connect with other living stones to become a living house.

In the Old Testament, the house, or temple, symbolized God's Presence with His people. The splendor of the place was the glory of God. Now we, individually and collectively as the church, are His temple (1 Cor. 6:19; 3:16). As shocking as it sounds, His glory is in us. Jesus said so (John 17:22). What does this mean?

There are two aspects of God's glory; external and internal. His *external* glory is the visible manifestation such as the glory cloud over the tabernacle (Exod. 40:34-35). James Boice explains that Jesus' *internal* glory "consists of his intrinsic worth, or character ... Thus, all that can be properly known of God is an expression of his glory ... When the disciples beheld his glory ... they actually beheld his character, which was the character of God."[3]

When Moses prayed, "Show me your glory," God replied, "I will make all my goodness pass before you" (Exod. 33:18-19). Then, when God passed by, He described His goodness, His attributes that are celebrated throughout the Old Testament and are embodied in Jesus.

The LORD descended in the cloud and stood with him there, and proclaimed the name of the LORD. The LORD passed before him and proclaimed, "The LORD, the LORD, a God merciful and gracious, slow to anger, and abounding in steadfast love and faithfulness, keeping steadfast love for thousands, forgiving iniquity and transgression and sin, but who will by no means clear the guilty, visiting the iniquity of the fathers on the children and the children's children, to the third and the fourth generation." (Exod. 34:5-7)

The goodness of His glorious character, His Holy Spirit, is in us. By His Word and His Spirit He transforms us into good people who are merciful, gracious, slow to anger, loving, faithful and forgiving. And the living house embodies what we have by grace been declared to be: "A chosen race, a royal priesthood, a holy nation, a people for his own possession" (1 Pet. 2:9).

This is our redeemed reality. However, petty irritations often trip me up. Malice and slander taste good. The bifurcated road looms large. The spiritual struggle to return to the Word and taste the goodness of Jesus is hard. I'm grateful that I'm part of a holy nation of people who have received mercy, so they extend mercy. They proclaim to me the excellencies of our Savior, remind me that the Lord is good and encourage me to trust and obey. And together we are transformed into a living house where the marvelous light of Glory shines to beckon people who are still in darkness.

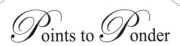

Points to Ponder

Is your appetite for God's Word increasing or decreasing?

How are you participating in a community of grace where you are encouraged and equipped to trust and obey God's Word?

Transformed by Prayer

Oh how I love your law!

It is my meditation all the day.

Your commandment makes me wiser than my enemies,

for it is ever with me ...

How sweet are your words to my taste,

sweeter than honey to my mouth!
(Ps. 119:97-98, 103)

Gracious Goodness: 1 Peter 2:12-25

Gracious words are like a honeycomb,
sweetness to the soul and health to the body.

(Prov. 16:24)

The discussion of submission does not begin with Peter's words to women in chapter 3. He begins this conversation by reminding us that our chief end is to glorify God.

Keep your conduct among the Gentiles honorable, so that when they speak against you as evildoers, they may see your good deeds and glorify God ... (1 Pet. 2:12).

Then he tells us, men and women, to submit: "Be subject for the Lord's sake to every human institution ... Live as people who are free, not using your freedom as a cover-up for evil, but living as servants of God" (1 Pet. 2:13-16).

Oddly, Peter juxtaposes *submission* and *freedom*. Isn't submission the antithesis of freedom? No, Jesus said, "If you abide in my word, you are truly my disciples, and you will know the truth, and the truth will set you free ... Everyone who practices sin is a slave to sin ... if the Son sets you free, you will be free indeed" (John 8:31-36).

This is not a subjective freedom. This is freedom to be what God created and redeemed us to be. Submission from the heart is the fruit of freedom in Christ. Submission "is a gracious thing, when, mindful of God, one endures sorrows while suffering unjustly ... But if when you do good and suffer for it you endure, this is a gracious thing in the sight of God" (1 Pet. 2:18-20).

"Gracious" is one of the attributes God revealed to Moses when He described His goodness (Exod. 34:5-7). Showing grace to others is not just improbable, it is impossible apart from the Cross; therefore, Peter tells us to "be mindful of God".

Be mindful of the *example* of Jesus: "For to this you have been called, because Christ also suffered for you, leaving you an example, so that you might follow in his steps" (1 Pet. 2:21).

Be mindful of the *substitutionary atonement* of Jesus: "He himself bore our sins in his body on the tree, that we might die to sin and live to righteousness" (1 Pet. 2:24).

In Gethsemane Jesus prayed, "My Father, if it be possible, let this cup pass from me; nevertheless, not as I will, but as you will" (Matt. 26:39). He voluntarily submitted to the Father's will in order to glorify Him by accomplishing our salvation. Freedom and submission met at the Cross. The power and grace of this love leaves us speechless. When we are consumed and compelled by His love, we gratefully submit to His will (John 14:15; 2 Cor. 5:14).

How do we live this way? The same way Jesus did — He *entrusted* Himself to the One who judges justly. And so should we.

When he was reviled, he did not revile in return; when he suffered, he did not threaten, but continued entrusting himself to him who judges justly. (1 Pet. 2:23)

Therefore let those who suffer according to God's will entrust their souls to a faithful Creator while doing good. (1 Pet. 4:19)

Moment by moment we hand over responsibility for ourselves to our faithful Creator. We stop trying to run our own, and other's lives. We don't have to earn approval because we are accepted in Christ. Self-protection is unnecessary because we are safe in Christ. We don't have to resist or fear earthly authorities because our hope is not in them. From this place of grace, our freedom in Christ is evidenced by our submission. Trust and obey. Gracious goodness.

Points to Ponder

What is your perspective of submission?

Is it shaped by God's Word?

Who are you entrusting your life to — right now?

Transformed by Prayer

You, O LORD, are a God merciful and gracious,

slow to anger and abounding in steadfast love and faithfulness.

Turn to me and be gracious to me;

give your strength to your servant ...

(Ps. 86:15-16).

Free to Submit: 1 Peter 2:24-3:7

Trust in the Lord with all your heart,
  and do not lean on your own understanding.
In all your ways acknowledge him,
  and he will make straight your paths.

(Prov. 3:5-6)

In 1 Peter chapter 3 Peter speaks specifically to women who were chosen and redeemed by Sovereign Grace. Don't let the chapter break deflect you from the potency of Peter's words. Just prior to his instructions to women he said, "He himself bore our sins in his body on the tree, that we might die to sin and live to righteousness ..." (1 Pet. 2:24). Then he continues: "Likewise, wives, be subject to your own husbands ... " (1 Pet. 3:1-2).

Likewise – like Jesus – use your freedom to submit to the Father's will. *Like Jesus,* when you are reviled, do not revile in return. *Like Jesus,* entrust your soul to your faithful Creator.

Some of the women in this passage were married to men who were not Christians. The congregation likely included single women and women married to believers. Whatever our marital status, Peter encourages us to remember the scope of the whole, reach up and grab the spiritual blessings that are ours in Jesus, and infuse the moment with His glorious grace. One way we do this is to graciously submit to those He puts in authority over us.

Mother Eve will teach us more about submission, but for now let's be clear. Submission is not easier for certain personalities and it was not easier in certain periods of history. Submission from the heart is unnatural because we are rebels. Submission is a work of grace. It is not a response to the character of one in authority over us. It is a response to Jesus' love and a reflection of His character. A woman is not to submit to sin. When she must refuse to submit, she can do so with a submissive and respectful heart. Submission is God's idea and it is good because He is good.

The desire and the will to do such a radical thing will not originate in the heart of one who is dead in sin. C. S. Lewis explains that there is a difference between biological life and spiritual life, and that a person who receives spiritual life "would have gone through as big a change as a statue which changed from being a carved stone to being a real man. And that is precisely what Christianity is about. This world is a great sculptor's shop. We are the statues and there is a rumour going through the shop that some of us are some day going to come to life."[4]

Peter calls the women to do something that is only possible for those who have "come to life". Outward expressions of submission are manipulative and controlling because they are motivated by self-interest. Free women have the capacity to submit from the heart because they have Life. Their power is God's grace and their motivation is His glory.

When we submit, our lives proclaim the excellencies of God. This submission is wordless. It's winsome. It's wise. It's on the inside yet it is so obvious that it cannot be denied by those who know us and eventually they begin to ask about the reason for the hope that is in us (1 Pet. 3:15). And we give them words of life.

Submission is not passive. It was the active obedience *of Jesus* that freed us from slavery to sin. It is our active obedience *to Jesus* that frees us to submit.

*P*oints to *P*onder

What difference does it make to see 1 Peter 3:1-7 in the context of chapters 1 and 2?

Is your submission like that of Jesus "who, though he was in the form of God, did not count equality with God a thing to be grasped, but emptied himself, by taking the form of a servant, being born in the likeness of men. And being found in human form, he humbled himself by becoming obedient to the point of death, even death on a cross"? (Phil. 2:6-8).

Transformed by Prayer

Search me, O God, and know my heart!

Try me and know my thoughts!

And see if there be any grievous way in me,

and lead me in the way everlasting!
(Ps. 139:23-24)

Transformed by Prayer

Search me, O God, and know my heart!

Try me and know my thoughts!

And see if there be any grievous way in me,

and lead me in the way everlasting!
(Ps. 139:23-24)

Beautiful Women: 1 Peter 3:1-7

Jesus, thy blood and righteousness my beauty are, my glorious dress;

'midst flaming worlds, in these arrayed, with joy shall I lift up my head.[5]

Nikolaus Ludwig von Zinzendorf

Peter clarifies his directives to women. He is not simply talking about outward behavior.

> *Do not let your adorning be external ... but let your adorning be the hidden person of the heart with the imperishable beauty of a gentle and quiet spirit, which in God's sight is very precious.* (1 Pet. 3:3-4)

Peter calls these "living stones" (1 Pet. 2:5) who have been " ... born again to a living hope through the resurrection of Jesus Christ ..." (1 Pet. 1:3), to adorn their hearts with the gospel. A rebellious heart is restless. A heart submitted to God is gentle and quiet. Jesus describes His own heart as "gentle and lowly" (Matt. 11:29).

The Greek word translated gentle "denotes gentle, mild, meek ... It is that temper of spirit in which we accept His dealings with us as good, and therefore without disputing or resisting ... This meekness, however, being first of all a meekness before God, is also such in the face of men, even of evil men, out of a sense that these, with the insults and injuries which they may inflict, are permitted and employed by Him for the chastening and purifying of His elect ... The meekness manifested by the Lord and commended to the believer is the fruit of power ... the Lord was 'meek' because he had the infinite resources of God at His command. Described negatively, meekness is the opposite to self-assertiveness and self-interest; it is equanimity of spirit that is neither elated nor cast down, simply because it is not occupied with self at all."[6]

In his book, *The Freedom of Self-Forgetfulness*, Tim Keller writes, "Because the essence of gospel-humility is not thinking more of myself or thinking less of myself, it is thinking of myself less ... [It] means I stop connecting every experience, every conversation, with myself. In fact, I stop thinking about myself. The freedom of self-forgetfulness. The blessed rest that only self-forgetfulness brings."[7]

The Greek word that is translated quiet "indicates tranquility arising from within, causing no disturbance to others."[8] Proverbs tells us, "A tranquil heart gives life to the flesh, but envy makes the bones rot" (14:30).

We are products of our theology. What we believe about God shows up every day in every situation and relationship. Peter illustrates this by pointing to fearless women who believed God's Word and the transforming difference this made in their lives.

> For this is how the holy women who hoped in God used to adorn themselves, by submitting to their husbands, as Sarah obeyed Abraham, calling him lord ... (1 Pet. 3: 5-6)

Eve and Sarah help us understand why submission is such a defining characteristic of a life-giver. Together they teach us why Peter expects such big things from us, because we have a big gospel that is powerful enough to transform us from life-takers to life-givers. So Peter moves our focus back to this live-giving gospel by reminding us that we are heirs of the grace of life.

> Likewise, husbands, live with your wives in an understanding way, showing honor to the woman as the weaker vessel, since they are heirs with you of the grace of life ... (1 Pet. 3: 7)

Liberated women, who live in the freedom of self-forgetfulness, have a life-giving beauty that is eternal.

Points to Ponder

Reflect on the big idea that our dead, sinful hearts can be transformed by God's grace into something that is alive with gentleness and quietness that is very precious to Him and life-giving to others.

Transformed by Prayer

Teach me, O LORD, the way of your statutes;

> *and I will keep it to the end.*

Give me understanding, that I may keep your law

> *and observe it with my whole heart.*

Lead me in the path of your commandments,

> *for I delight in it.*

Incline my heart to your testimonies,

> *and not to selfish gain!*

Turn my eyes from looking at worthless things;

> *and give me life in your ways.*
>
> (Ps. 119:33-37)

Living Covenantally: 1 Peter 3:8-22

> And the LORD said to him, "I have heard your prayer and your
> plea, which you have made before me. I have consecrated this
> house that you have built, by putting my name there forever. My
> eyes and my heart will be there for all time."
>
> (1 Kings 9:3)

Suffering does not exempt us from the privileges and
responsibilities of covenant life.

> Finally, all of you, have unity of mind, sympathy, brotherly love,
> a tender heart, and a humble mind. Do not repay evil for evil
> or reviling for reviling, but on the contrary, bless, for to this you
> were called, that you may obtain a blessing ... For the eyes of the
> Lord are on the righteous, and his ears are open to their prayer.
> ... (1 Pet. 3:8-9, 12)

The covenant community is a *called* community of people who
are not defined by their suffering – even though suffering is part
of life – but by their relationship with the One who always sees
and hears them.

The Westminster Confession of Faith makes a startling statement
about covenant life in God's family. It explains that those who
are united to Christ are also "united to one another in love,
they have communion in each other's gifts and graces, and are
obliged to the performance of such duties, public and private,
as do conduce to their mutual good ..."[9]

We are *united* and *obliged*. These strong words are counter-
intuitive and counter-cultural, but this is what Jesus prayed for
us: "The glory that you have given me I have given to them, that
they may be one even as we are one, I in them and you in me,
that they may become perfectly one ..." (John 17:22-23).

Our covenant union with Christ ignites our covenant love
for His other children. Our positional unity is a gift of grace.
Our privilege and responsibility are to nurture this unity in
practical ways so that our local churches are vibrant witnesses
of the transforming power of the gospel. Peter gives a stunning
summary of the gospel.

For Christ also suffered once for sins, the righteous for the unrighteous, that he might bring us to God, being put to death in the flesh but made alive in the spirit. (1 Pet. 3:18)

Peter becomes doxological as he points to the eschatological reality of Christ's rule and reign — the now and not yet of our redemption.

[Jesus] has gone into heaven and is at the right hand of God, with angels, authorities, and powers having been subjected to him. (1 Pet. 3:22)

The Cross and the Consummation compel elect exiles to live covenantally and to let that quiet, redemptive beauty transform the culture of our home, church, and world.

And now, let's look back to the beginning and ask Mother Eve to disciple us by sharing the gospel and her life with us. It's the covenant way.

 oints to onder

Have you seriously considered that your union with Christ unites you to His other adopted children?

How are you nurturing covenant family life in your church?

Transformed by Prayer

Remember me, O LORD, when you show favor to your people;

help me when you save them,

that I may look upon the prosperity of your chosen ones,

that I may rejoice in the gladness of your nation,

that I may glory with your inheritance.

(Ps. 106:4-5)

THREE

Eve in Eden

Genesis 1–2

ELLEN'S STORY

Ellen Dykas is the Women's Ministry Coordinator for Harvest USA, a national organization focused on church education and discipleship regarding gospel-centered sexuality. She lives in Philadelphia, Pennsylvania.

In my years of ministry to hundreds of women mired in the pain, confusion and shame usually attached to sexual sin, I've learned so much! One key truth is that all women are much more alike, than different. We need Jesus and we all face temptations to look away from Him for love, life, satisfaction and security. Like any other sin, sexual sin is active participation in what God admonished His people about in Jeremiah 2:13: turning away from Him as the fountain of living waters and striving to dig our own wells of water; seeking to find life outside of Christ. When the daughters of God ignore, despise or are merely unaware of our identity in Him, and our unique redemptive calling as women, we're just as prone as men are to seek sexual experiences and self-crafted identities as a way of making life "work".

A colleague spoke at a national conference for college students, addressing "Homosexuality and Faith". As the workshop wound down, a young woman raised her hand to share about the heartache of her past experiences of living under a gay identity, and many homosexual relationships. The lack of peace and joy in her own life had softened her to God's pursuit. In her distress, David White tells how, "God surrounded her with Christian friends whose lives looked so different. They had the contentment and shalom her life sorely lacked. Resonating with what I taught about God's design, she concluded with a profound point about our sexuality: because God is the life-giver, homosexual activity can't fit his plan because it will never produce life."[1]

Sexual sin, with men, women, self, technology or in our thoughts, are evidences that our hearts have been hijacked by unbelief from God's beautiful design of women. He alone is life, and He alone gives life to His loved daughters who are then sent out to give that life away!

THINKING BIBLICALLY

"The Greatest Story Ever Told" – this title has been used for the Bible, and with good reason. The Bible is the greatest storybook not just because it is full of wonderful stories but because it tells one great story, the story of Jesus ... Only God's revelation could maintain a drama that stretches over thousands of years as though they were days or hours. Only God's revelation can build a story where the end is anticipated from the beginning, and where the guiding principle is not chance or fate, but promise ... Only God can shape history to a real and ultimate purpose. The purpose of God from the beginning centers on His Son.[2]

Edmund P. Clowney

Genesis 1

¹*In the beginning, God created the heavens and the earth*

²*The earth was without form and void, and darkness was over the face of the deep. And the Spirit of God was hovering over the face of the waters.*

³*And God said, "Let there be light," and there was light.*

⁴*And God saw that the light was good.*

- What do you learn about God?
- What is the imperative in verse 3?
- In what ways is God bringing order out of chaos in your life? Or, how do you need Him to do this?

When designing a house, an architect considers structurally and aesthetically how to build a strong and beautiful dwelling. Then the builder follows the architect's blueprints. Genesis 1–3 are God's divine blueprints for all of life.

In Genesis 1 and 2 we see two grand cornerstones. The first is that God is our reference point, the place we run when we must make choices, or when life falls apart. The second cornerstone is that God's Word is our authority. When He said, "Let there be light," light obeyed.

²⁶*Then God said, "Let us make man in our image, after our likeness. And let them have dominion over the fish of the sea and over the birds of the heavens and over the livestock and over all the earth and over every creeping thing that creeps on the earth."*

²⁷*So God created man in his own image, in the image of God he created him; male and female he created them.*

²⁸*And God blessed them. And God said to them, "Be fruitful and multiply and fill the earth and subdue it and have dominion over the fish of the sea and over the birds of the heavens and over every living thing that moves on the earth."*

- What do you learn about yourself?
- What do you think it means to be God's image-bearer?

- How are the cultural mandate (Gen. 1:28) and the gospel mandate (Matt. 28:18-20) related?

- How is God giving you opportunities to tell His story and share His glory as an image-bearer?

An image stamped on a coin signifies authority. God created the man and woman to be ambassadors of His authority by ruling and reigning over creation as His vice-regents. God created them male and female to reflect the community and distinctiveness of the Triune Him. Maleness and femaleness puts God's story and glory on display.

God gave man and woman a mission to be fruitful and multiply, to go and be life-givers, to spread Eden to the ends of the earth.

Genesis 2

⁷then the LORD God formed the man of dust from the ground and breathed into his nostrils the breath of life, and the man became a living creature.

⁸And the LORD God planted a garden in Eden, in the east, and there he put the man whom he had formed.

¹⁵The LORD God took the man and put him in the garden of Eden to work it and keep it.

¹⁶And the LORD God commanded the man, saying, "You may surely eat of every tree of the garden,

¹⁷but of the tree of the knowledge of good and evil you shall not eat, for in the day that you eat of it you shall surely die."

- What do you learn about the man?

In Genesis 2, we see the detailed and dirty description of the creation of man and woman. Man/Adam is created first. He is a glorious blend of humility and dignity. In humility, God forms man from the ignoble dust. In dignity, the supreme Life-giver breathes life into man's nostrils. He gives a place called Eden. He gives a mission called work. He gives protection through loving boundaries. And yet, there is a stark contrast, a gaping hole, a piece is missing, for the first time God declares something "not good".

¹⁸Then the LORD God said, "It is not good that the man should be alone; I will make him a helper fit for him."

²¹So the LORD God caused a deep sleep to fall upon the man, and while he slept took one of his ribs and closed up its place with flesh.

²²And the rib that the LORD God had taken from the man he made into a woman and brought her to the man.

- What did God say was not good?

A new design plan is unveiled. Woman is not taken from the earth but from the side of man, signifying a close and intimate bond. She solves the problem that no animal could – aloneness. She is God's provision for human community. She is like man, but not identical to him. She is his complement. Her mission is to be an ezer, the Hebrew word for helper. Ezer is used to describe the ministry of God and of woman. Ezer points to strong, relational, life-giving qualities. God created man in such a way that he needs an ezer to help him accomplish his mission. We, too, need an ezer to provide what is lacking to accomplish our mission.

> [23]Then the man said, "This at last is bone of my bones and flesh of my flesh; she shall be called Woman, because she was taken out of Man."

> [24]Therefore a man shall leave his father and his mother and hold fast to his wife, and they shall become one flesh.

> [25]And the man and his wife were both naked and were not ashamed.

- What astonishes you about this passage?
- According to Ephesians 5:22-33, what does marriage illustrate?

God performs the first wedding ceremony and two become one. He places the bride and groom in the first sanctuary, made so by His Presence there. The groom highlights the intimacy of this union and communion with his words "Bone of my bones and flesh of my flesh". We are urged toward covenantal commitment by the challenge to "hold fast". Authenticity and transparency are celebrated by the words "naked and unashamed." This pinnacle of oneness and Presence points to our final Eden – the New Heaven and New Earth — with our Heavenly Bridegroom. Astonishing is an understatement.

LIVING COVENANTALLY

God's very existence is covenantal: Father, Son, and Holy Spirit live in unceasing devotion to each other, reaching outward beyond the Godhead to create a community of creatures serving as a giant analogy of the Godhead's relationship. Created in the image of the Triune God, we are by nature outgoing, interdependent relationship establishers, finding ourselves in the other and not just in ourselves ... We were not just created and then given a covenant; we were created as covenant creatures – partners not in deity, to be sure, but in the drama that was about to unfold in history.[3]

Michael Horton

The Beginning: Genesis 1:1-3

In the beginning was the Word [Jesus], and the Word was with God, and the Word was God. He was in the beginning with God. All things were made through him, and without him was not anything made that was made.

(John 1:1-3)

Eve, the first woman to walk on planet earth, is the prototype. We cannot understand our femaleness without understanding her, but the story did not begin with her. This is God's Story and it began before the beginning.

Let's use our biblically informed imaginations and pretend we were there ...

Before the beginning, we watch the Father, Son, and Holy Spirit live in glorious goodness, love and unity. We know something extraordinary is about to happen when we hear the Triune One make a covenant of redemption.

Blessed be the God and Father of our Lord Jesus Christ ... he chose us in him before the foundation of the world ... to the praise of his glorious grace. (Eph. 1:3-6)

We hear the Son agree to redeem those the Father chose.

In him we have redemption through his blood ... so that we who were the first to hope in Christ might be to the praise of his glory. (Eph 1:7, 12)

And we hear the Holy Spirit agree to apply this redemption to the hearts of the ones the Father chose and the Son redeemed.

... [You] were sealed with the promised Holy Spirit, who is the guarantee of our inheritance until we acquire possession of it, to the praise of his glory. (Eph 1:13-14)

We know the Father, Son and Holy Spirit are *equal* in power and glory and share a *common* purpose, to praise His glorious grace (Gen 1:6, 12, 14). So we are fascinated that each assumes a *different* function in this redemption plan, yet their perfect equality is not compromised.

We see the formless void, and we watch "the Spirit of God hovering over the face of the waters" (Gen. 1:2).

Hover, a strong, tender word, suggests the movement of a bird. The Spirit protects the mass of emptiness "Like an eagle that stirs up its nest, that flutters over its young, spreading out its wings, catching them ..." (Deut. 32:11).

We cannot imagine what will happen but we know it will reflect the glory and goodness of the *Triune Him.* We hold our breath, and then ... "God said, "Let there be light," and there was light (Gen. 1: 3).

The blinding beauty overwhelms us. The formless void begins to be transformed into shapes and colors.

"Let there be light" happened in my (Susan's) life when I was twenty-two. God sovereignly placed me in a Christian family with a rich legacy of faith. I was the good church girl and assumed my heritage and goodness would get me to heaven, but being good was exhausting and empty. Then, in a Bible class, God said, "Let there be light" and in that light, I saw His goodness and my wretchedness. By His grace, I was separated from darkness and transferred to light. After the initial euphoria, I wondered why no one told me the gospel before. As the Holy Spirit renewed my mind I realized, they *did* tell me, but it was not until God opened my blind eyes and deaf ears that I could see and hear. Then I was speechless as I realized that during those years I tried to earn my way to heaven, the Spirit of God hovered over me. After more than fifty years I'm still awestruck that God created and redeemed me to dwell in the light of His Presence.

Points to Ponder

When did God say "Let there be light" in your life?

What are your thoughts about the Spirit hovering over you when you were walking in darkness?

Transformed by Prayer

Bless the LORD, O my soul!

    O LORD my God, you are very great!

You are clothed with splendor and majesty,

covering yourself with light as with a garment,

    stretching out the heavens like a tent.

        O LORD, how manifold are your works!

In wisdom have you made them all; ...
                                  (Ps. 104:1-2, 24).

Transformative Truths: Genesis 1:3-31

Not to us, O LORD, not to us, but to your name give glory,
for the sake of your steadfast love and your faithfulness!

(Ps. 115:1)

Volumes have been written about Genesis 1, but we simply want to consider four truths that transform our view of God, ourselves and the world.

#1: God's Word is our authority, whether we recognize it or not. "God said, 'Let there be light,' and there was light" (Gen. 1:3). God commanded and light obeyed. Light did what it was created to do.

#2: God's glory is our purpose. "Then God said, 'Let us make man in our image, after our likeness'" (Gen 1:26). Human beings were created to live in God's presence — in a unique relationship with Him — and to reflect some aspects of His glory and goodness.

#3: Gender distinctiveness is God's good plan. "So God created man in his own image ... male and female he created them" (Gen. 1:27). This view is known today as complementarianism. *Women's Ministry in the Local Church* explains:

> *Complementarianism gives the relational framework for men and women to live out their covenantal privileges and responsibilities. The complementarian position acknowledges that God created men and women equal in being but assigned different – but equally valuable – functions in His kingdom and that this gender distinctiveness complements, or harmonizes, to fulfill His purpose.*

> *Complementarians believe that the Bible teaches that God has created men and women equal in their essential dignity and human personhood, but different and complementary in function – with male spiritual leadership in the home and believing community, the Church, being understood as a part of God's design. That means that both men and women are image-bearers*

of the living God. We are each fully human in all that entails. We are equals before the cross, brothers and sisters in our Lord Jesus Christ. But God has made us different ... [4]

#4: Gender distinctiveness is necessary to fulfill the cultural mandate to be fruitful, multiply and have dominion over the earth. "And God blessed them. And God said to them, 'Be fruitful and multiply and fill the earth and subdue it and have dominion ...'" (Gen, 1:28).

The man and woman had the same authority, purpose and mandate — but they were different by God's design. And that difference is very good. God said so. "And God saw everything that he had made, and behold, it was very good" (Gen. 1:31).

This is the way life is supposed to be. We were created to trust and obey God's Word, live in His presence, and reflect Him to each other and to the world. This is the good life.

Points to Ponder

Which of the four foundational truths are counter-cultural?

*Are they counter-intuitive to you or are they
transforming your thoughts and actions?*

Transformed by Prayer

I will extol you, my God and King,

> *and bless your name forever and ever.*

Every day I will bless you

> *and praise your name forever and ever. ...*

One generation shall commend your works to another,

> *and shall declare your mighty acts.*

On the glorious splendor of your majesty,

> *and on your wondrous works, I will meditate.*
>
> (Ps. 145:1-5)

By Design: Genesis 2

> Q. 12. What special act of providence did God exercise toward man in the estate wherein he was created?
>
> A. When God had created man, he entered into a covenant of life with him, upon condition of perfect obedience; forbidding him to eat of the tree of the knowledge of good and evil, upon the pain of death.[5]
>
> Westminster Shorter Catechism

Genesis 1 is a fast-paced presentation of the scope of creation. In Genesis 2 the narrative zooms in on God's creation of the man and woman. There is a significant shift from *God (Elohim)*, referring to Him as the transcendent Creator, to *LORD God (Yahweh)*, His personal name indicating that He lives in covenant relationship with His people.

> ... then the LORD God formed the man of dust from the ground and breathed into his nostrils the breath of life, and the man became a living creature. (Gen. 2:7)

God created man first, thus assigning him the role of headship.

> The LORD God took the man and put him in the garden of Eden to work it and keep it. And the LORD God commanded the man, saying, "You may surely eat of every tree of the garden, but of the tree of the knowledge of good and evil you shall not eat, for in the day that you eat of it you shall surely die." (Gen. 2:15-17)

God designed the man to work and keep, to provide and protect, so that he could fulfill the responsibilities of headship. God entered into a covenant with Adam as the representative of all his descendants. Adam's obedience meant life; disobedience meant death. Immediately after designating Adam to be the representative for mankind in this covenant, God declared that man's aloneness was not good.

> Then the LORD God said, "It is not good that the man should be alone; I will make him a helper fit for him." (Gen 2:18)

In God's tender "I will" we see His sovereign initiative in providing what man needed to help him fulfill his noble, self-sacrificing calling.

Aloneness was not good because man was created in the image of the Triune God. He needed one who was equal but different so that their complementarity would reflect the equality and diversity of the Trinity. Wayne Grudem explains:

> In 1 Corinthians 11 Paul writes, "But I want you to understand that the head of every man is Christ, the head of a wife is her husband, and the head of Christ is God". (v. 3)
>
> We can say then that a relationship of authority and submission between equals, with mutual giving of honor, is the most fundamental and most glorious interpersonal relationship in the universe."[6]

Now we begin to see why Peter put such emphasis on submission. Submission is not a result of the curse. It preceded sin. It does not indicate an inferior function. Christ's function in redemption is not inferior to the Father's. Headship and submission are woven into the fabric of creation. This is God's ordained order for enjoying oneness in marriage and unity in the church that reflects the unity and diversity of the Trinity. When men and women in God's covenant family value their own design and the design of the opposite sex, God is glorified.

*P*oints to *P*onder

What are some of your observations about boys/men that show their "provide/protect" design?

How does their maleness enable them to be servant-leaders in the home and church?

How does your femaleness enable you to help others glorify God?

Do you celebrate gender differences?

Transformed by Prayer

O Lord, you have searched me and known me!

You know when I sit down and when I rise up;

you discern my thoughts from afar ...

For you formed my inward parts;

you knitted me together in my mother's womb.

I praise you, for I am fearfully and wonderfully made.

Wonderful are your works;

my soul knows it very well.

(Ps. 139:1-2, 13-14)

Helper: Genesis 2:18

And I will ask the Father, and he will give you another Helper, to be with you forever, even the Spirit of truth, whom the world cannot receive, because it neither sees him nor knows him. You know him, for he dwells with you and will be in you.

(John 14:16-17)

Men and women were created to be God's image-bearers. As His female image-bearers, we were designed to be helpers.

Then the Lord God said, "It is not good that the man should be alone; I will make him a helper fit for him." (Gen. 2:18)

This design is not limited to woman's role as a wife. If it was, then a woman would have to be married to reflect God's design. No one is married their entire life, and some people never marry. Our design is certainly applicable to marriage but is bigger than marriage.

The Hebrew word for helper, *ezer*, is frequently used in Scripture to refer to God as our Helper. Read the following verses and write a brief description beside each one of how God helps us. Then consider how you can be a helper in your relationships.

*May he send you help from the sanctuary
and give you support from Zion! (Ps. 20:2)*

*Our soul waits for the LORD;
he is our help and our shield. (Ps. 33:20)*

*God is our refuge and strength,
a very present help in trouble. (Ps. 46:1)*

*Behold, God is my helper;
the Lord is the upholder of my life. (Ps. 54:4)*

*For he delivers the needy when he calls,
the poor and him who has no helper. (Ps. 72:12)*

You, LORD, have helped me and comforted me. (Ps. 86:17)

The LORD is on my side as my helper;
I shall look in triumph on those who hate me. (Ps. 118:7)

I was pushed hard, so that I was falling,
but the LORD helped me. (Ps. 118:13)

(See also: Ps. 10:14; Ps. 70:5; Ps. 94:17-18.)

Of course God helps men and women, and men and women are to help others, but it does seem that women are uniquely designed for this relational, nurturing, caring ministry of help.

Georgia Settle, the first Coordinator of Women's Ministry for the Presbyterian Church in America, was one of our spiritual mothers. One of our favorite memories is when she told our women's ministry committee that we were frapping cables. We were not impressed, until she explained that while her husband was preparing to preach on Acts 27, he made a discovery. She read verses 14-17:

> *But soon a tempestuous wind, called the northeaster, struck down from the land. And when the ship was caught and could not face the wind, we gave way to it and were driven along. Running under the lee of a small island called Cauda, we managed with difficulty to secure the ship's boat. After hoisting it up, they used supports to undergird the ship. ...*

The Greek word translated "supports" (*boethia*) is also translated "help", "rope", or "supporting cables". The nautical term for these ropes is frapping cables. They were used on wooden ships to keep them from breaking apart in rough waters. The point? *Boethia* is the same as the Hebrew word *ezer*.

Helper is an exceptional design with an essential function.

Peter tells women that we will be daughters of Sarah if we "do good and do not fear anything that is frightening" (1 Pet. 3:6). How can we be good and fearless when the ship is about to break apart?

> *For he has said, "I will never leave you nor forsake you." So we can confidently say, "The Lord is my helper; I will not fear; what can man do to me?"* (Heb. 13:5-6).

Points to Ponder

Has there been a time when you were going through rough waters and a woman was a frapping cable for you? How did she help you?

Transformed by Prayer

May all who seek you

rejoice and be glad in you;

may those who love your salvation

say continually, "Great is the LORD!"

As for me, I am poor and needy,

but the LORD takes thought for me.

You are my help and my deliverer;

do not delay, O my God!

(Ps. 40:16-17)

The First and Last Marriage: Genesis 2:21-24

Let us rejoice and exult and give him the glory, for the marriage of the Lamb has come, and his Bride has made herself ready ... Blessed are those who are invited to the marriage supper of the Lamb.
(Rev. 19:7, 9)

Marriage is a sacred covenant, a holy relationship between a man and a woman that was instituted by God. Even if a person is not married, he/she needs to understand God's plan and purpose for marriage because marriage is about more than the couple saying "I do".

Marriage is God's idea. The woman was His gift to the man and Adam responded, "At last!"

So the LORD God caused a deep sleep to fall upon the man, and while he slept took one of his ribs and closed up its place with flesh. And the rib that the LORD God had taken from the man he made into a woman and brought her to the man. Then the man said,

"This at last is bone of my bones
and flesh of my flesh,
she shall be called Woman,
because she was taken out of Man." (Gen. 2:21-23)

He named her, showing his headship. He named her Woman, showing their equality.

Therefore a man shall leave his father and his mother and hold fast to his wife, and they shall become one flesh. (Gen 2:24)

Paul quotes this verse in Ephesians 5 and then explains: "This mystery is profound, and I am saying that it refers to Christ and the church" (v. 32). Marriage is an exquisite illustration of the relationship between Jesus and His Bride, the church.

When a man loves, cherishes, cares for, and protects his wife, he illustrates Jesus' headship over His church.

When a woman respectfully submits to her husband's headship, she illustrates the church's submission to Christ.

And when one falters, the other is *not* exempt from fulfilling his/her covenant responsibility to be an image-bearer of God in the marriage.

Neither man nor woman can obey these gospel imperatives in their own strength, but the Holy Spirit motivates and empowers us to fulfill our covenant vows. God's grace transforms two individual people into one so that with one heart and voice they glorify God as husband and wife. As they grow in oneness, their marriage begins to point to the profound mystery of the gospel – our oneness with the Lord Jesus.

When a man and woman say "I do", from that day forward they have the sacred privilege and responsibility to illustrate the most glorious thing in the universe; the love of Christ for His church. They have the potential to point to what is truly ultimate, the gospel of our Lord and Savior. Their "my story" will not just become an "us story", it will be a gospel story.

Perhaps the sweetest moment of a wedding is when the doors open and the bride and groom have their "first look" at each other. Their joy is unbridled. Marriage is to be treasured and protected, not just by those who are married but by every member of Christ's church as we wait for that sacred moment when the doors of heaven open and we see our Bridegroom. With the veil removed, we will see the scope of the whole story of redemption and how every part of our story worked together to bring us to this glorious consummation.

Points to Ponder

*Do you see yourself as a bride,
regardless of your marital status?*

How are you getting ready for that "first look"?

Transformed by Prayer

How precious is your steadfast love, O God!

The children of mankind take refuge in the shadow of your wings.

They feast on the abundance of your house,

and you give them drink from the river of your delights.

For with you is the fountain of life;

in your light do we see light.

Oh, continue your steadfast love to those who know you,

and your righteousness to the upright of heart!

(Ps. 36:7-10)

FOUR

Eve in Exile

Genesis 3–4

HELEN'S STORY

In one of her books, Noel Piper tells about Helen Roseveare, a missionary doctor who went to Africa in 1953. Noel quotes the following from Helen's own writings.

"Things had gone wrong at Nebobongo. I was very conscious that my life was not what it should have been. I was losing my temper with nurses, being impatient with the sick, getting irritated with workmen ... I was overwhelmingly tired, with an impossible work load and endless responsibilities.

"The day came when ... I snapped at a woman patient. A small incident grew out of all proportion ... [Everyone] listened in horrified amazement to the Christian missionary doctor, as she lost her temper in fluent Swahili ...

"[Pastor Ndugu] had seen my spiritual need and made all the arrangements for me to go to stay in his village for a long weekend ... I sought God's face for two unhappy days, but I could find no peace ... Sunday evening, Pastor Ndugu called me out to the fireside where he and his wife, Tamoma, were sitting ... We prayed ... Opening his Bible at Galatians 2:20, he drew a straight line in the dirt floor with his heel. 'I,' he said, 'the capital I in our lives, Self, is the great enemy ... the trouble with you is that we can see so much Helen that we cannot see Jesus.'

"... My eyes filled with tears.

"'I notice that you drink much coffee ... When they bring a mug ... you stand there holding it, until it is cool enough to drink. May I suggest that every time, as you stand and wait, you should just lift your heart to God and pray ... ' and as he spoke, he moved his heel in the dirt across the I he had previously drawn, '... Please, God, cross out the I.'

There in the dirt was his lesson of simplified theology – the Cross – the crossed-out I life ... 'I have been crucified with Christ and I no longer live, but Christ lives in me'" (Gal. 2:20).[1]

THINKING BIBLICALLY

This gracious promise (Gen. 3:15) becomes an organizing theme for the rest of Scripture and the rest of human history, as every character and event find their place in relation to the great battle that now unfolds between the conquering Seed of the woman and the resistance of Satan.[2]

Gospel Transformation Bible

Genesis 3

Genesis 2 concludes with a stunning statement of life in Eden: "And the man and his wife were both naked and were not ashamed" (v. 25). No shame. All good. Until ...

> ¹*Now the serpent was more crafty than any other beast of the field that the LORD God had made. He said to the woman, "Did God actually say, 'You shall not eat of any tree in the garden'?"*
>
> ²*And the woman said to the serpent, "We may eat of the fruit of the trees in the garden,*
>
> ³*but God said, 'You shall not eat of the fruit of the tree that is in the midst of the garden, neither shall you touch it, lest you die.'"*
>
> ⁴*But the serpent said to the woman, "You will not surely die ...*
>
> ⁶*she took of its fruit and ate, and she also gave some to her husband who was with her, and he ate.*
>
> ⁷*Then the eyes of both were opened, and they knew that they were naked. And they sewed fig leaves together and made themselves loincloths.*

- What did the serpent tempt woman to do?
- Was woman a helper to her husband?

The excellent wife of Proverbs 31 "does him good, and not harm, all the days of her life" (v. 12).

Adam's *helper* became his *harmer*. Adam became a covenant-breaker. They both became sinners. Their eyes were opened, but what they saw was their corruption.

It should have ended. It would have ended, except ... before creation the Triune God made a covenant of redemption, and He is a covenant keeper.

> ⁸*And they heard the sound of the LORD God walking in the garden in the cool of the day, and the man and his wife hid themselves from the presence of the LORD God among the trees of the garden.*
>
> ⁹*But the LORD God called to the man and said to him, "Where are you?"*

- How do verses 8-9 tell the gospel story?

From this moment forward, this will be the story — us hiding and God seeking. "For the Son of Man came to seek and to save the lost" (Luke 19:10).

> [10]And he said, "I heard the sound of you in the garden, and I was afraid, because I was naked, and I hid myself."

> [11]He said, "Who told you that you were naked? Have you eaten of the tree of which I commanded you not to eat?"

> [12]The man said, "The woman whom you gave to be with me, she gave me fruit of the tree, and I ate."

> [13]Then the LORD God said to the woman, "What is this that you have done?" The woman said, "The serpent deceived me, and I ate."

- Who did Adam protect?
- Who did he blame?
- Underline Adam's "I" statements in verse 10.

Woman's protector hid *himself* and accused *her*. His self-generated solution left them cowering as the Lord God spoke to the serpent.

> [14]"Because you have done this, cursed are you above all livestock and above all beasts of the field; on your belly you shall go, and dust you shall eat all the days of your life.

> [15]I will put enmity between you and the woman, and between your offspring and her offspring; he shall bruise your head, and you shall bruise his heel."

- Underline God's "I" statement.

With a death sentence ringing in the air, God sovereignly declares life. Embedded in this prophecy of the conflict between the seed of the Serpent and the Seed of the woman is the first revelation of the covenant of grace — the promise of an

Offspring who would destroy Satan. This is the promise Peter said holy women hope in.

The covenant of grace is the sovereignly initiated arrangement by which the Triune God lives in saving favor and merciful relationship with His people. There was grace; however, there would also be consequences for their sin, and some consequences would be gender-specific.

> [16]*To the woman he said, "I will surely multiply your pain in childbearing; in pain you shall bring forth children. Your desire shall be for your husband, and he shall rule over you."*

- What are some words that describe the emotional pain in biological and spiritual mothering?

Woman would experience the pain of seeing her children sick, sorrowing, fighting, rebelling and dying. Her relationship with her husband would be hard. Before sin, she joyfully and willingly submitted to him. Now she would struggle in her soul and resist his headship. "Desire" is the same word used in Genesis 4:7: "Sin is crouching at the door. Its desire is for you, but you must rule over it." Just as sin desires to possess and control us, a wife desires to possess and control her husband.

> [17]*And to Adam he said, "Because you have listened to the voice of your wife and have eaten of the tree of which I commanded you, 'You shall not eat of it,' cursed is the ground because of you; in pain you shall eat of it all the days of your life*
>
> [18]*thorns and thistles it shall bring forth for you; and you shall eat the plants of the field.*
>
> [19]*By the sweat of your face you shall eat bread, till you return to the ground, for out of it you were taken; for you are dust, and to dust you shall return."*

Work is not the curse. Work was given before the Fall. The curse is that work will be hard. The ground will be full of thorns and thistles. The fall brought death and it would return him to dust. A thorny and thistly life would be filled with prickly problems, trials and discouragements. We will not have Eden on earth, but God promised a way back to the Garden. There are consequences for sin but there is also a Cross. Adam believed the promise and responded in faith.

²⁰*The man called his wife's name Eve, because she was the mother of all living.*

Eve means *life-giver*. Her name is a celebration of the promise that through a woman the Life of the world would come.

²¹*And the LORD God made for Adam and for his wife garments of skins and clothed them.*

²²*Then the LORD God said, "Behold, the man has become like one of us in knowing good and evil. Now, lest he reach out his hand and take also of the tree of life and eat, and live forever—"*

²³*therefore the LORD God sent him out from the garden of Eden to work the ground from which he was taken.*

- They are exiles, but they are elect exiles, pilgrims looking for the promise. They have battled two of the three great enemies of our soul; the flesh and the devil. Now Adam and Eve will confront the assault of the world outside of Eden. Make a list of the "knowns" of Eden and the "unknowns" outside of Eden.

- How has God shown Himself faithful as He has moved you from the known to the unknown?

- List three reasons you are thankful that the gospel allows you to live eyes wide open, naked and unashamed.

LIVING COVENANTALLY

The more excellent way of loving-kindness, hesed, is to govern our relationships in the Christian community. This is not sappy sentimentalism. Biblical love is a reflection of the character of Jesus. It is a fruit of grace.[3]

Susan Hunt & Barbara Thompson

Deformation: Genesis 3

... all have sinned and fall short of the glory of God.
(Rom. 3:23)

We don't know how long the man and woman lived in the perfection of Eden before the cosmic scandal that rocked their world, but we do know the consequences thundered throughout creation and tumbled all the way down to you and me.

Therefore, just as sin came into the world through one man, and death through sin, and so death spread to all men because all sinned (Rom. 5:12)

It seems so innocent ... a beautiful creature in their beautiful garden. He approaches the woman first and tempts her to doubt God's Word. The road divides and she ignores God's creation order and acts independently. The Deceiver ratchets up the conversation and flat-out contradicts God's Word.

In *A Sacred Sorrow*, Michael Card writes, "Adam and Eve enjoyed the unbroken Presence of God. It was immediate and intimate. His *hesed*, an untranslatable Hebrew word often rendered 'loving-kindness,' was a given, reliable as the fresh, newly created air they both breathed. Then ... Satan the Accuser and ultimate cause of all lament, called into question the *hesed* of God."[4] Distrust and disobedience caused the deformation of the image of God in Adam and the woman. Instantly they moved from "naked and not ashamed" to a ridiculous and desperate attempt to cover their shame.

When they became their own authority, they reflected their selfishness rather than God's *hesed* to each other. It was devastating and deadly. They trusted self rather than God. Woman became a life-taker.

They watched the shining one become the slithering one. As shame swirled around woman's heart, she must have listened fearfully to the curse conveyed upon her accuser. He who once appeared so tantalizing was humbled to eat dirt. Sin had broken shalom and hostility would reign in relationships.

We live in a society that is captivated by "i". Steve Jobs used this branding from the beginning of Apple. He said the "i" stood for, "valuable things, like individual, imagination, or i as in me."[5] Man and woman began spouting off "I" statements as soon as they were naked. The oneness of "we" was shattered by sin and replaced by "I" and "me". Interdependence was exchanged for independence. Sin causes us to justify self and avoid God.

Sin distorts manhood and womanhood. Motherhood would be painful spiritually, emotionally and physically. Woman's relationship to her husband would look more like a tug o' war than tranquility. Her inclination would be to dominate rather than submit. His default would be to rule in harshness rather than humility.

Imagine their surprise when they heard the promise of a life-giver encased in a curse. Paul tells of a " … God of peace who will soon crush Satan …" (Rom. 16:20). This is the hope that Adam and Eve, and the women Peter referred to as holy heirs of the grace of life, anticipated.

Points to Ponder

*How does the enemy deceive you by asking,
"Did God actually say ... ?"*

How does he tempt you to doubt God's loving-kindness?

*What are the consequences when you listen to lies
and distrust God's Word?*

What surprises you about God's grace?

Transformed by Prayer

Have mercy on me, O God,

according to your steadfast love;

according to your abundant mercy

blot out my transgressions.

Wash me thoroughly from my iniquity,

and cleanse me from my sin!

(Ps. 51:1-2).

Transformation: Genesis 3:15-21

For the wages of sin is death, but the free gift of God is eternal life in Christ Jesus our Lord.

(Rom. 6:23)

The man and woman deserved *death* but they heard a promise of *life* as God spoke to the serpent.

I will put enmity between you and the woman, and between your offspring and her offspring; he shall bruise your head, and you shall bruise his heel. (Gen. 3:15)

God's "I will" is a statement of sovereign initiative that resounds through Scripture and into our hearts. It is His promise to do for us what we cannot do for ourselves. This is a covenant of grace. We cannot earn it and do not deserve it.

The man called his wife's name Eve, because she was the mother of all living. (Gen. 3:20)

Naming, a privilege of headship, was forfeited when Adam disobeyed God. The gospel restored manhood and the privilege of naming. Eve is post-fall and pre-biological motherhood, but she is declared to be a life-giver. This redemptive calling is more than biological. Every redeemed woman can be transformed from life-taker to life-giver in every relationship and situation. She has the capacity to do good instead of harm. The exponential potential of her mission to be fruitful and multiply has been restored.

In the next scene, God does not simply *tell* them how this transformation will occur. He *shows* them.

The LORD God made for Adam and for his wife garments of skins and clothed them. (Gen. 3:21)

Adam and Eve had heard of death but had never seen it. The horror of watching blood flow from the lifeless animal must have been crushing. An innocent substitute died so they could be covered. And it was God who killed the animal. His *hesed* for them was irrevocable, irresistible and transforming.

... Behold, the Lamb of God, who takes away the sin of the world! (John 1:29)

... without the shedding of blood there is no forgiveness of sins. (Heb. 9:22)

I will greatly rejoice in the LORD *... for he has clothed me with the garments of salvation; he has covered me with the robe of righteousness...* (Isa. 61:10)

... our citizenship is in heaven, and from it we await a Savior, the Lord Jesus Christ, who will transform our lowly body to be like his glorious body, by the power that enables him even to subject all things to himself. (Phil. 3:20-21)

𝒫oints to 𝒫onder

What are some reasons you rejoice in your robe of righteousness?

When have you seen women being life-takers?

When have you seen them being life-givers?

How is God transforming you from life-taker to life-giver?

Transformed by Prayer

For I know my transgressions,

and my sin is ever before me.

Against you, you only, have I sinned

and done what is evil in your sight,

so that you may be justified in your words

and blameless in your judgment.

Behold, I was brought forth in iniquity,

and in sin did my mother conceive me.

Behold, you delight in truth in the inward being,

and you teach me wisdom in the secret heart.

Purge me with hyssop, and I shall be clean;

wash me, and I shall be whiter than snow.

(Ps. 51:3-7)

Transforming Movement: Genesis 4

Q. 35. What is sanctification?

A. Sanctification is the work of God's free grace, whereby we are renewed in the whole man after the image of God, and are enabled more and more to die unto sin, and live unto righteousness.[6]

Westminster Shorter Catechism

Adam and Eve were expelled from Eden, but they were *elect* exiles.

It would seem that sanctification would be easy for Eve. She had lived in perfection with the Perfect One. But our depravity is so ... well, *total*. Sin infects the mind, emotions and will. Sanctification was hard for her, just as it is for us, because death to self is slow.

Now Adam knew Eve his wife, and she conceived and bore Cain, saying, "I have gotten a man with the help of the LORD." (Gen. 4:1)

Twenty-four verses later there is a fundamental difference in her perspective.

And Adam knew his wife again, and she bore a son and called his name Seth, for she said, "God has appointed for me another offspring instead of Abel, for Cain killed him." (Gen. 4:25).

In the first statement, Eve begins with herself, "*I* have done this." In the Garden, Eve made the prideful decision to be her own authority. As an elect exile, she reverted to her original sin.

In the second statement, Eve's reference point is God. This movement from an "I" orientation to a "God" orientation is the transformation from life-taker to life-giver.

At least three things happened between these two births to cause such a profound change.

... she bore his brother Abel ... And when they were in the field, Cain rose up against his brother Abel and killed him. (Gen. 4:2-8)

First, Eve saw the son she took such pride in murder his brother. Sin was more horrific than she could have imagined.

*The L*ORD *said to Cain, "Where is Abel your brother?" He said, "I do not know; am I my brother's keeper?"* (Gen. 4:9)

Second, two contrasting ways of life, caused by the conflict between the seed of the Serpent and the Seed of the woman, came into sharp focus: The way of Cain and the way of Christ. The way of Cain is strident independence centered on "I". The way of Christ is characterized by interdependent relationships of keeping, or caring, for one another.

*Then Cain went away from the presence of the L*ORD *and settled in the land of Nod, east of Eden.* (Gen 4:16)

When the road divided, Cain rejected God's authority. The way of Cain is a restless existence of self-rule. Nod means wandering. Christ-followers gather together under the authority of God's Word.

Cain knew his wife, and she conceived and bore Enoch. When he built a city, he called the name of the city after the name of his son, Enoch. (Gen. 4:17)

The follower of Cain builds his own city for his own glory. The chief end of Christ-followers is God's glory.

Cain is the poster-child for those who turn away from God.

... Jesus, who saved a people out of the land of Egypt, afterward destroyed those who did not believe. ... Woe to them! For they walked in the way of Cain ... (Jude 5, 11)

Third, Eve saw the emptiness and ugliness of women pursuing outward beauty.

And Lamech took two wives. The name of the one was Adah, and the name of the other Zillah. (Gen. 4:19)

Adah and Zillah, the first women mentioned after Eve, agreed to polygamy and pursued the superficial. Adah means pleasure, beauty, to decorate. Zillah means shade. According to James

Boice, this may refer to "a luxuriant covering of hair ... Here was a culture committed to physical pleasure, beauty, and charm and not to those inner qualities that Peter describes as being 'the unfading beauty of a gentle and quiet spirit, which is of great worth in God's sight'" (1 Pet. 3:4).[7]

After a lot of suffering, and a lot of grace, there was a radical change in the orientation of Eve's life. Eve's suffering was not a deterrent to her forward movement; it was actually the means to remove the "I" and to adorn her heart with the gospel.

Points to Ponder

How are the circumstances of your life moving you away from self-sufficiency and to the sufficiency of God's grace (2 Cor. 12:9)?

Transformed by Prayer

Let me hear joy and gladness;

let the bones that you have broken rejoice.

Hide your face from my sins,

and blot out all my iniquities.

Create in me a clean heart, O God,

and renew a right spirit within me.

Cast me not away from your presence,

and take not your Holy Spirit from me.

Restore to me the joy of your salvation,

and uphold me with a willing spirit.

Then I will teach transgressors your ways,

and sinners will return to you.

(Ps. 51:8-13)

Clinging Women: Psalm 119:25

My soul clings to the dust;
give me life according to your word!

The life of Christ in us gives us the *capacity* to be life-givers. The struggle is being a life-giver in *practice. Becoming* a life-giver is a gift of grace; *being* a life-giver is a life-long process of clinging to Christ rather than clinging to self. Augustus Toplady's desperate words in the hymn *Rock of Ages* should be our song:

Nothing in my hand I bring, simply to thy cross I cling;
Naked, come to thee for dress;
Helpless, look to thee for grace;
Foul, I to the Fountain fly; wash me, Savior, or I die.[8]

Were these Eve's thoughts when she looked at her nakedness? Was she repulsed by her hands that had grasped what was forbidden? When she realized her helpless and hopeless condition, then heard God's promise to free her from the Deceiver, did she haltingly hold out empty hands? When she heard the promise of a Deliverer, did she fly ... did she plead, "Wash me, Savior, or I die"?

Outside the Garden, when she began clinging to self again, how often did she pray "I cling to your testimonies, O LORD; let me not be put to shame!" (Ps. 119:31)?

This is not just about Eve. This is about us. When we cling to self we cling to dust. We know our propensity to self-sufficiency, but God is good and He remembers that we are dust.

The LORD is merciful and gracious,
slow to anger and abounding in steadfast love.
He will not always chide,
nor will he keep his anger forever.
He does not deal with us according to our sins,
nor repay us according to our iniquities.
For as high as the heavens are above the earth,
so great is his steadfast love toward those who fear him;
as far as the east is from the west,
so far does he remove our transgressions from us.

> As a father shows compassion to his children,
>> so the LORD shows compassion to those who fear him.
> For he knows our frame;
>> he remembers that we are dust. (Ps. 103:8-14)

We, too, need to remember that we are dust and pray: "My soul clings to you; your right hand upholds me" (Ps. 63:8).

In the *Women's Devotional Bible*, Ann Voskamp writes:

The Hebrew word used for "clings" (v. 8) is the same Hebrew word used in Genesis 2:24: "Therefore a man shall leave his father and his mother and hold fast to his wife." If our soul clings to God, it holds fast to God not only in intimacy but in promised obedience. There is no experience of God unless there is obedience to God.[9]

We cling to our dusty self, but the life of Christ in us empowers us to loosen our grip on the dust and cling to glory. And slowly we are transformed from dust to glory.

$\mathcal{P}$oints to $\mathcal{P}$onder

And we all, with unveiled face, beholding the glory of the Lord, are being transformed into the same image from one degree of glory to another. For this comes from the Lord who is the Spirit. (2 Cor. 3:18)

Right now,
regardless of what is going on in your life,
are you clinging to dust or to glory?

Transformed by Prayer

O God, you are my God; earnestly I seek you;

my soul thirsts for you; my flesh faints for you,

as in a dry and weary land where there is no water.

So I have looked upon you in the sanctuary,

beholding your power and glory.

Because your steadfast love is better than life,

my lips will praise you ...

for you have been my help,

and in the shadow of your wings I will sing for joy.

My soul clings to you;

your right hand upholds me.

(Ps. 63:1-3, 7-8)

Trust and Obey: 1 Peter 4:19

Trust and obey, for there's no other way
To be happy in Jesus, but to trust and obey.[10]

John Sammis

Adam represented us in the covenant of works. He was a covenant-breaker. He did not trust and obey. Jesus is our representative in the covenant of grace. His perfect trust and obedience secured our salvation. Our obedience does not *earn* our salvation; it is *evidence* of our salvation. We obey the one we trust.

> *Therefore let those who suffer according to God's will entrust their souls to a faithful Creator while doing good.* (1 Pet. 4:19)

We obey the one we love. "If you love me, you will keep my commandments" (John 14:15).

Sin distorts God's image in us. Now it's unnatural for us to trust and obey anyone other than self. God's loving purpose is to restore the image of His Son in us. "For those whom he foreknew he also predestined to be conformed to the image of his Son ..." (Rom. 8:29).

John brilliantly explains what is involved in this transformation: "He must increase, but I must decrease" (John 3:30).

If "I" decreases, but nothing fills that space, there is emptiness. The increasing Presence of Jesus in our hearts drives out the "I". This is what Thomas Chalmers, the nineteenth-century Scottish theologian, famously described as "the expulsive power of a new affection".

As Eve fought her "I", did she remember the Garden where she rebelliously trusted self rather than God? Did her eyes of faith focus on the promised Offspring who, in another Garden, would trust and obey God in order to redeem her?

When she reflected on the tree of the knowledge of good and evil, did she lean forward in faith to see another tree of good and evil ... one where all of her evil was poured out on the only Good One, where "He himself bore our sins in his body on the tree, that we might die to sin and live to righteousness ..." (1 Pet. 2:24)?

The death of "I" is painful and slow, but it's a death that brings Life and Love. It's a grueling, glorious, messy, marvelous transformation. No short-cuts. No formulas. It is moment-by-moment trusting the Triune God who loved me before creation and will love me for all eternity. It is moment-by-moment obeying His Word. The hymn writer John Sammis instructs:

> When we walk with the Lord in the light of His Word,
> What a glory he sheds on our way! While we do his good will,
> He abides with us still, and with all who will trust and obey.

So I fight the "I" in me with the weapons God provides. I take " ... the sword of the Spirit, which is the word of God, praying at all times in the Spirit ..." (Eph. 6:17-18) and I ask the Spirit to use His sword to hack away the "I" in my heart. Then I bravely look "I" in the eye and say, "Bring it on, whatever you throw at me will be used to conform me to the likeness of Jesus. Change it up, confuse me, bully me. The Power *in* me is stronger than the power *of* me and by His grace I will trust and obey Him." Then I ask myself life-giving questions:

- What will it mean to glorify God in this situation/relationship?

- What will it mean to bring this situation/relationship under the authority of God's Word rather than my feelings?

- Are there any ways I am being a life-taker?

- What will it mean to be a life-giver?

- How can my sisters help me, and how can I help them, to be a life-giver?

That's a day in the life of a life-giver, no matter what the day looks like.

Points to Ponder

*Who do you trust with the relationships
and circumstances in your life?*

*In what ways have you minimized God's work
and trusted your own efforts?*

*Who is increasing and who is decreasing
in your heart?*

Transformed by Prayer

Deliver me from bloodguiltiness, O God,

O God of my salvation,

and my tongue will sing aloud of your righteousness.

O LORD, open my lips, and my mouth will declare your praise.

For you will not delight in sacrifice, or I would give it;

you will not be pleased with a burnt offering.

The sacrifices of God are a broken spirit;

a broken and contrite heart, O God, you will not despise.
(Ps. 51:14-17)

FIVE

Sarah's Story
Genesis 11–12

CHANDRA'S STORY

Chandra Oliver is an IT Business Systems Analyst and Chaplain Wife. Originally from Oklahoma City, her husband is currently stationed at Fort Carson.

Today I am sitting in a military chapel and sweet sisters surround me, filling the pews with their presence and laughter. We have much in common. We attend Bible study together, we live in the same housing communities, we shop at the same grocery store, we get coffee at the same Starbucks, we move every few years, we have endured combat deployments, we have sweet memories of homecomings, we have closets with black dresses for the inevitable funerals war brings, and the list continues.

In the midst of these sisters, my thoughts wander to one striking way I am unlike these women. I do not have children. I am "barren". That is a difficult word to write. Encircled by conversations about play-dates and developmental milestones I listen, I smile, I engage, and I am reminded that I am different, the outcast. Rapidly my thoughts spiral downward; soon my emotions follow my thoughts. As I mourn my empty arms, silence stops my internal dialogue as my eyes are drawn to the stained glass windows. In this moment, the Holy Spirit gently reminds me of Philippians 4:8, " ... fill our minds with beauty and truth ... " In this instant, I wonder, "What is beautiful or true?"

Then comes a tap on my shoulder as a friend asks me to hold her infant. Brought back into the moment, I realize I am surrounded by Beauty and Truth. My covenant family surrounds me, my sisters surround me, and my *daughters* surround me. I am not the "outcast"; rather, I am a mother in Israel. I was specifically created to enter into the lives of women. Just as a biological mother invests her life into her children, I too have the opportunity to raise up the next generation that they might love the Almighty, care for their husbands, and nurture their children in faith. I gladly die to self so these daughters might know more of the One who loves them. They are my inheritance.

THINKING BIBLICALLY

God blesses Abram to be a blessing bearer. The procreative intentions of divine blessing are always within the context of loyalty to the spiritual transformation of future generations.[1]

Bruce Waltke

Genesis 11

¹Now the whole earth had one language and the same words

³And they said to one another, "Come, let us make bricks ...

⁴let us build ourselves a city and a tower with its top in the heavens, and let us make a name for ourselves, lest we be dispersed over the face of the whole earth."

*⁶And the L*ORD *said ... ⁷"Come, let us go down and there confuse their language, so that they may not understand one another's speech."*

*⁸So the L*ORD *dispersed them from there over the face of all the earth ...*

⁹Therefore its name was called Babel ...

²⁷Now these are the generations of Terah. Terah fathered Abram, Nahor, and Haran ...

²⁹And Abram and Nahor took wives. The name of Abram's wife was Sarai ...

³⁰Now Sarai was barren; she had no child.

- Underline the "let us" statements in verses 1-3.
- What was their objective?
- Underline God's "let us" statement in verse 7.
- What was God's objective? (See Gen. 1:28, Matt. 28:18-20.)
- Circle the word that describes Sarai's condition.

Thus we are introduced to Sarah (God changes her name later in the narrative) who was married to a key figure in God's redemption story. "By faith Abraham obeyed when he was called to go out to a place that he was to receive as an inheritance. And he went out, not knowing where he was going" (Heb. 11:8). He "believed God, and it was counted to him as righteousness" (Gal. 3:6). Jesus' genealogy in Matthew traces salvation back to Abraham (Matt. 1:1). Zechariah said Jesus' birth fulfilled God's promise to Abraham (Luke 1:68, 72-73). Luke writes that in Abraham's "offspring shall all the families of the earth be blessed" (Acts 3:25). He is called the father of the faith (Acts 7:1-3) and the friend of God (2 Chron. 20:7; Isa. 41:8; James 2:23). And "he was looking forward to the city that has foundations, whose designer and builder is God" (Heb. 11:10).

Babel typifies the *Way of Cain* — independence, self-rule, and self-glory that results in division and destruction.

Sarai's barrenness stands in stark contrast to the cultural mandate to be fruitful and multiply. Barrenness shouts of being empty, parched or depleted and yet it is a void that holds the promise of being filled. Walter Brueggemann writes:

> There is no real genesis or new beginning for barren people apart from God ... To stay in safety is to remain barren, to leave is to have the promise of hope ... departure from securities is the only way out of barrenness.[2]

Genesis 12

¹Now the LORD said to Abram, "Go from your country and your kindred and your father's house to the land that I will show you.

²And I will make of you a great nation, and I will bless you and make your name great, so that you will be a blessing.

³I will bless those who bless you, and him who dishonors you I will curse, and in you all the families of the earth shall be blessed."

⁴So Abram went, as the LORD had told him, and Lot went with him. Abram was seventy-five years old when he departed from Haran.

⁵And Abram took Sarai his wife ... and they set out to go to the land of Canaan.

- What is the command?
- Underline God's "I will" statements.
- What do you learn about God, our Covenant Maker?
- Read Hebrews 11:1 and 6 and 2 Corinthians 5:7: What do you learn about faith?
- Read Hebrews 11:8-12: List the things Abraham and Sarah did by faith.

The covenant of grace, announced in Genesis 3:15, progressively unfolds throughout the Old Testament. In the Abrahamic covenant, God sovereignly initiates a relationship with this pagan couple and establishes the holy nation, through whom the Promised One will come and in whom all the families of the earth shall be blessed. He promises to make their name great, as opposed to those in the way of Cain who sought to make a name for themselves. He promises to bless them and that their lives will be a conduit of blessing to others. The Sovereign source of these blessings promises life to a barren couple and a home to homeless people.

Abraham and Sarah were not seeking God but were chosen by God. This sets up the continuing contrast between the *Way of Cain* and the *Way of Christ.* The people at Babel trusted self-effort; Abraham and Sarah will trust God's promise. God scattered the people at Babel; He will gather a new nation, a chosen race (1 Pet. 2:9), through Abraham and Sarah.

The genesis of this story mirrors the genesis of creation. God created a promise out of the nothingness in an elderly barren couple. He replaces the chaos of Babel with the order of a new name and nation. He declares the promise that He is the God who forms and fills barren and void places. He moves Abraham and Sarah from the known to the unknown. To *go* means to *leave,* to determinedly disassociate oneself. To cut all ties. To embrace the life of an elect exile, alien and sojourner. Sarah is silent, choosing not to whine, complain or drag her feet. In her silence, she yields and submits to go.

Like our first parents, and Abraham and Sarah, we are called to pilgrim life. When the road divides between the known and the unknown, we must trust the natural or the supernatural. We must walk by sight or by faith in the God who has made Himself known. Walking by faith is a journey towards transformation.

> [6]*Abram passed through the land to the place at Shechem, to the oak of Moreh. At that time the Canaanites were in the land.*
>
> [7]*Then the LORD appeared to Abram and said, "To your offspring I will give this land." So he built there an altar to the LORD, who had appeared to him.*
>
> [8]*From there he moved to the hill country on the east of Bethel and pitched his tent, with Bethel on the west and Ai on the east. And there he built an altar to the LORD and called upon the name of the LORD.*

- Underline God's promise.
- Underline Abraham's response.

A pilgrimage is a sacred journey. Abraham and Sarah were not city-builders like Cain and the people at Babel. They were altar-builders because they knew that "here we have no lasting city, but we seek the city that is to come" (Heb. 13:14).

When these progressing pilgrims arrived in Canaan, they did what elect exiles do. They believed God's promise, built an altar and called on the name of the Lord. They claimed the place for God and bore witness that "everyone who calls on the name of the Lord will be saved" (Rom. 10:13), even though "the Canaanites were in the land". Their sojourn points us to the path our Promise Keeper took. He left home by faith. He was obedient to His Father. He was sacrificed on the altar. He went to the Promised Land to prepare a place for us.

LIVING COVENANTALLY

The unity here proposed [in John 17:20-21] is of persons specially given to Jesus by the Father. Not, then, of all men who happen to dwell in any particular province, district, or city, but a unity of persons who have received, not common life as all have, but life eternal ... brought into vital union with the person of the Lord Jesus ... persons to whom God's name has been manifested; people who have seen what others never saw.[3]

Charles Spurgeon

Growing in Knowledge: Romans 12:2

The Bible does tell us who we are and what we should do, but it does so through the lens of who God is. The knowledge of God and the knowledge of self always go hand in hand.[4]

Jen Wilkin

Peter's statement about Sarah has huge theological implications.

... Sarah obeyed Abraham, calling him lord. And you are her children, if you do good and do not fear anything that is frightening. (1 Pet. 3:6)

Have you ever wondered why God designates Sarah, rather than Eve, as our spiritual mother? If we look at this verse in a vacuum, and not in the context of the gospel, we can come to some whacky conclusions. *If I call my husband lord I will be a daughter of Sarah, whatever that means!* As we study Sarah's story, we'll explore the significance of being her children.

The Old Testament stories progressively show the grace of God pulsating through history; they show us Jesus. God tells us His Story by giving us stories of people. Through these stories we see how He keeps the promise of Genesis 3:15 to provide a Redeemer. In God's revelation of Himself to His people, He makes Himself known so we can know Him and "be transformed by the renewal of your mind" (Rom. 12:2).

In his classic work *Knowing God*, J. I. Packer writes:

What were we made for? To know God.
What aim should we set ourselves in life? To know God.
What is "eternal life" that Jesus gives? Knowledge of God.
"This is eternal life: that they may know you, the only true God, and Jesus Christ, whom you have sent" (John 17:3).
... Once you become aware that the main business that you are here for is to know God, most of life's problems fall into place of their own accord.[5]

God's grace that gives us a *saving* knowledge of Christ also empowers our continued education in the knowledge of Him. God gives us His Holy Spirit who "will teach you all things

142

and bring to your remembrance all that I have said to you"
(John 14:26).

As we journey with Sarah, we will see how God progressively
makes Himself known to her. As we hear her story, the overriding
question is: How does knowing Sarah's story help us know God
better?

How are you pursuing a deeper knowledge of God?

How are you using the means of grace He has provided
– His Word, prayer, worship, the sacraments–
to know Him better?

Transformed by Prayer

Forever, O LORD, your word

is firmly fixed in the heavens.

Your faithfulness endures to all generations;

you have established the earth, and it stands fast.

By your appointment they stand this day,

for all things are your servants.

If your law had not been my delight,

I would have perished in my affliction.

I will never forget your precepts,

for by them you have given me life.

I am yours; save me,

for I have sought your precepts.

(Ps. 119:89-94)

The Call: Genesis 12:1-4

His divine power has granted to us all things that pertain to life and godliness, through the knowledge of him who called us to his own glory and excellence ...

(2 Pet. 1:3)

God's call to Abraham in Genesis 12:1-3 was also a call on Sarah's life. This call is so familiar that it's easy to glide over it without pondering the magnitude of the moment. Abraham was a seventy-five-year old pagan with a sixty-five-year old barren wife when it happened. Surely he told her about this experience. I wonder about her reaction. The imperative to "Go" is jarring. Then there was the promise of a great nation. Did she go into panic mode: *Children? I'm barren. I'm old. Who will bear these children for my husband?* Did the impossibility paralyze her with fear? Sometimes the Gospel is terrifyingly disruptive. How could Abraham comfort his wife? What would quieten her spirit? Like us, she needed to know the Promise Maker (the Father) and the Promise Keeper (Jesus).

As jaw-dropping as the promise is, the first four words are equally so. "Now the LORD said" (Gen 12:1) is totally unexpected. God had not spoken to a man since Noah. Now He speaks to a pagan and reveals Himself as *Yahweh,* the God of covenant faithfulness who lives in personal relationship with His people. Here we begin to see the structure of a covenant as God sovereignly initiates a relationship with Abraham and obligates Himself to him: *I will* show you, *I will* make of you, *I will* bless you, *I will* protect you.

The imperative to go and be a blessing is given in the context of the change God makes in Abraham's status: *I will bless you.* This imperative reaches back to the cultural mandate (Gen. 1:28) and forward to the gospel mandate to "Go" and take dominion by making disciples (Matt. 28:19-20). All that God promises to do for, with, and through Abraham is accomplished through the gospel promise in Genesis 3:15.

Know then that it is those of faith who are the sons of Abraham. And the Scripture, foreseeing that God would justify the Gentiles by faith, preached the gospel beforehand to Abraham, saying, "In you shall all the nations be blessed." So then, those who are of faith are blessed along with Abraham, the man of faith. (Gal. 3:7-9)

When God speaks in His Word He reveals *Himself* to His people. The unfolding of His Word "gives light; it imparts understanding to the simple" and those who love it have "great peace ... nothing can make them stumble" and they respond, "my heart stands in awe of your words" (Ps. 119:130, 165, 161).

Did Abraham stand in awe that *God spoke*? Was Sarah in awe that God spoke to *her* husband? What was their response?

Does seeing Jesus in all of Scripture leave you awestruck?

What difference does the knowledge that God initiated a relationship with you make in your life?

Transformed by Prayer

The sum of your word is truth,

and every one of your righteous rules endures forever.

Princes persecute me without cause,

but my heart stands in awe of your words

(Ps. 119:160-161)

The Response: Genesis 12:4-5

... I count everything as loss because of the surpassing worth of knowing Christ Jesus my Lord. ...

(Phil. 3:8)

Scripture gives no indication that Sarah balked about leaving the luxurious port city of Ur. We stagger at the complexity of emotions and plans needed to prepare to cross the Arabian Desert and go to an unknown destination, but with extraordinary simplicity we are told, "So Abram went, as the LORD had told him, and ... took Sarai his wife ..." (Gen. 12:4-5).

Their obedience is stunning, but it is not the cause of their faith; it is evidence of their faith. Where did this faith come from?

Notice the order of events as Abraham and Sarah become part of the redemption story:

Now Sarai was barren ... (Gen. 11:30).
Now the LORD said to Abram, "Go ..." (Gen. 12:1).
So Abram went ... (Gen 12:4).

Barrenness is certainly not a punishment, but it is a painful and profound illustration of our fallenness. We are dead in sin. We cannot change our barren status. The barren motif keeps popping up in the redemption narrative — Rebekah, Rachel, Hannah, and Elizabeth — as reminders of our deadness and God's grace. He speaks Life into our deadness.

And I will give you a new heart, and a new spirit I will put within you. And I will remove the heart of stone from your flesh and give you a heart of flesh. And I will put my Spirit within you, and cause you to walk in my statutes and be careful to obey my rules. (Ezek. 36:26-27)

The Triune God changes our status from dead in sin to alive in Christ. What an amazing, undeserved, unmerited, transforming exchange.

So Abram went. Of course he did. Grace is irresistible. And Sarah went with him. Obedience is the response of a heart of flesh.

150

If we miss this order, we are prone to simply make much of Abraham and Sarah. Their faith and obedience are without doubt inspiring, but even the faith is a gift from God.

> *And you were dead in the trespasses and sins in which you once walked, ...*
> *But God, being rich in mercy, because of the great love with which he loved us,*
> *even when we were dead in our trespasses, made us alive together with Christ ... For by grace you have been saved through faith. And this is not your own doing; it is the gift of God, not a result of works, so that no one may boast.* (Eph. 2:1-2, 4-5, 8-9)

The faith God gives us has the capacity to do things we would never consider when our hearts were dead. Dr. James Boice writes:

> Biblical faith is simply believing God and acting on that belief, as Abram did ... When we talk about faith in God ... we are talking about faith in one whose nature and ways are beyond our full rational comprehension. As a result, what God commands often seems contrary to reason. Faith is not irrational, of course ... If God is God and if he is the kind of God he has demonstrated himself to be in his acts of both creation and redemption, then it is the most rational thing in the world to believe him ... If we look to circumstances or argue in terms of possibilities, God's promises always seem beyond our belief—simply because God is beyond our comprehension and his plans for us are always beyond our present experience.[6]

Peter tells us that Sarah hoped in God, submitted to her husband, and did not fear something that was frightening, even though it was far beyond anything she had ever experienced. This is the reasonable response of one who is alive in Christ. The luxury of Ur has lost its grip.

Points to Ponder

*It's easy to say we believe in God, but are there areas of your
life where it is frightening to act on that belief?*

*Meditate on the surpassing worth of knowing
Christ Jesus your Lord.*

*What desert will you have to cross
to know Him better?*

Transformed by Prayer

Your testimonies are my heritage forever,

for they are the joy of my heart.

I incline my heart to perform your statutes

forever, to the end.

(Ps. 119:111-112)

Building Altars: Genesis 12:6-9

May grace and peace be multiplied to you in the knowledge of God and of Jesus our Lord.

(2 Pet. 1:2)

Like Abraham and Sarah, we are pilgrims living in the now of barrenness and the hope of a promise yet to be. We know that one day we will see "the holy city, new Jerusalem, coming down out of heaven from God, prepared as a bride adorned for her husband" and we will hear "a loud voice from the throne saying, 'Behold, the dwelling place of God is with man. He will dwell with them, and they will be his people, and God himself will be with them as their God'" (Rev. 21:2-3).

So we claim each place where we are sovereignly placed — our home, neighborhood, workplace, hospital room, school — for God's glory and we proclaim the gospel with words and without words.

Beloved, I urge you as sojourners and exiles to abstain from the passions of the flesh, which wage war against your soul. Keep your conduct among the Gentiles honorable, so that when they speak against you as evildoers, they may see your good deeds and glorify God on the day of visitation ... Likewise, wives, be subject to your own husbands, so that even if some do not obey the word, they may be won without a word by the conduct of their wives, when they see your respectful and pure conduct. (1 Pet. 2:11-12; 3:1-2).

As we journey with Sarah from Ur to Canaan, I am struck by what is *not* recorded. Traveling through a desert is hot, boring, exhausting and dangerous, but there is no evidence that she whined, cajoled or questioned Abraham's decision. Sometimes being a life-giver is as much about what we *don't do* as what we do, what we *don't say* as what we say. A spirit that is quiet because of our knowledge of God's sovereignty responds by building altars and sacrificing expectations and comforts (Rom. 12:1-2).

As we continue to travel with Sarah, we see that like Eve, and like us, her sanctification is slow. But through every experience, side-trip and delay God was with her, sovereignly working everything together to accomplish His purpose. Her story dazzles us with God's persevering love for His chosen ones. His sovereignty assures us that He *can* keep His promises and His love assures us that He *will*. This knowledge is, indeed, powerfully transforming.

Points to Ponder

What are some ways you can claim the places you are placed for God's glory?

How can you proclaim the gospel without words in your current situation and relationships?

How does a pilgrim perspective help you to be a life-giver?

Transformed by Prayer

I will extol you, O LORD, for you have drawn me up

and have not let my foes rejoice over me.

O LORD my God, I cried to you for help,

and you have healed me ...

You have turned for me my mourning into dancing;

you have loosed my sackcloth and clothed me with gladness,

that my glory may sing your praise and not be silent.

O LORD my God, I will give thanks to you forever!
(Ps. 30:1-2, 11-12)

Faltering Faith/Forever Faithful: Genesis 12:10-20

... I have loved you with an everlasting love; therefore I have continued my faithfulness to you.

(Jer. 31:3)

If I had never read Genesis 12, I would *not* have seen this coming. I would have expected that after such life-altering obedience Abraham and Sarah would live happily-ever-after. But "there was a famine in the land" (Gen. 12:10).

They were where God told them to be when the crisis came. The promise contradicted their perceived reality: family/childless, land/none, blessing/famine. Maybe the altar-building had become routine ritual. Maybe they were tired and discouraged. You can almost hear Satan whispering, "Did God really say ... ?" The road divides. "So Abram went down to Egypt to sojourn there, for the famine was severe in the land" (Gen 12:10).

In the Bible, Egypt stands for the world. "Woe to those who go down to Egypt for help ... but do not look to the Holy One of Israel or consult the LORD!" (Isa. 31:1).

It gets worse.

When he was about to enter Egypt, he said to Sarai his wife, "I know that you are a woman beautiful in appearance, and when the Egyptians see you, they will say, 'This is his wife.' Then they will kill me, but they will let you live. Say you are my sister, that it may go well with me because of you, and that my life may be spared for your sake". (Gen. 12:11-13)

This forces some questions: Did Sarah's submission help Abraham trust and obey God? What would biblical submission mean in this situation?

When Abram entered Egypt, the Egyptians saw that the woman was very beautiful. And when the princes of Pharaoh saw her, they praised her to Pharaoh. And the woman was taken into Pharaoh's house. (Gen 12:14-15)

If the marriage with Pharaoh was consummated, the continuity of the covenant would be broken. But that *could not, would not* happen because this covenant does not depend on man. This is a covenant of grace that depends on God's promise to provide and protect. He has bound Himself to us in covenant loyalty.

> *But the LORD afflicted Pharaoh and his house with great plagues because of Sarai, Abram's wife. So Pharaoh called Abram and said, "What is this you have done to me? Why did you not tell me that she was your wife? Why did you say, 'She is my sister,' so that I took her for my wife? Now then, here is your wife; take her, and go." And Pharaoh gave men orders concerning him, and they sent him away with his wife and all that he had.* (Gen 12:17-20)

The pattern of the Garden is repeated. Just like our first parents, Abraham and Sarah trusted self. The air around them is filled with shame and guilt. We, too, look to Egypt and complicate our lives through disobedience. But God protects and preserves His promise. Sarah is untouched. The Egypt episode showed Abraham and Sarah, and us, that God's love is "patient and kind," it always protects, and it "never ends" (1 Cor. 13:4, 8).

I have another question: If the one I trusted to protect me abandoned me, would the conversation as we traveled back to Canaan be life-giving or life-taking? The question reveals my problem. The One I should ultimately trust is the only One who can promise to never leave me or forsake me.

> *For the mountains may depart*
> *and the hills be removed,*
> *but my steadfast love shall not depart from you,*
> *and my covenant of peace shall not be removed,"*
> *says the LORD, who has compassion on you.* (Isa. 54:10)

The more we "See what kind of love the Father has given to us, that we should be called children of God ..." (1 John 3:1), the more robustly we proclaim:

> *The steadfast love of the LORD never ceases;*
> *his mercies never come to an end;*
> *they are new every morning;*
> *great is your faithfulness.* (Lam. 3:22-23)

If this happens, even a little, Egypt is not a wasted trip. Our sanctification is slow and sloppy, but God's love is steadfast and sure.

$\mathscr{P}$oints to $\mathscr{P}$onder

*How have your side-trips to Egypt shown you God's
persevering, loyal love for you?*

*What is your reaction to the assurance
of God's forever faithfulness to you?*

Transformed by Prayer

You have dealt well with your servant,

O LORD, according to your word.

Teach me good judgment and knowledge,

for I believe in your commandments.

Before I was afflicted I went astray, but now I keep your word ...

It is good for me that I was afflicted,

that I might learn your statutes.

The law of your mouth is better to me

than thousands of gold and silver pieces.

(Ps. 119:65-67, 71-72)

SIX

Sarah's Sanctification
Genesis 15–17

RONJANETT'S STORY

Ronjanett Taylor is the State Director for an AmeriCorps literacy tutoring program serving K-3 students in twenty-six Mississippi elementary schools. She lives in Jackson, Mississippi.

I was given a legacy of faith by the women in my family as they lived out the helper characteristic of "seeing and caring for the oppressed" (Ps. 10:14). They showed me the importance of connecting care for a person's physical needs with their spiritual needs and inspired a desire to point people to the gift of eternal life in Christ and a life of commitment to him. But it was not until I was thirty-one years old that I began to understand the theological foundation for such life-giving living.

Our blended family moved to Mississippi. As newly-weds, in a new place, new to the Presbyterian Church in America, and separated from family, we experienced the faithfulness of God who transformed us through our transitions. The Lord used His people to show us covenant life as we brought the rich traditions of our faith and African-American culture into service and ministry in our church. We experienced great love and developed close and lasting friendships that made us feel like family.

In this context, we heard the sound preaching of God's Word and learned that covenant community life is an overflow of God's covenant relationship with His people. At a Women's Ministry Leadership conference, Karen Hodge spoke on "Gospel-Centered Community" and I learned that the Holy Spirit empowers us to live covenantally.

I have experienced challenging circumstances in life, family, and ministry – fractured relationships, parenting adult children, changes in church leadership, and struggling with self-doubt. But greater than the challenges has been the gift of God's Word and His people showing me the life-giving power of prayer, honest and hard admission of sin, bearing the burdens of others, looking beyond personal ability to seek help and being willing to ask for and extend forgiveness.

Then I was asked to share my testimony. Writing my story helped me realize *why* my biological and covenant family live as they do. God's electing, persevering, transforming love empowers and motivates us to be life-givers.

THINKING BIBLICALLY

[Genesis 15:6] is perhaps the most important verse in the entire Bible.[1]

James Boice

Genesis 15

*¹After these things the word of the L*ORD *came to Abram in a vision: "Fear not, Abram, I am your shield; your reward shall be very great."*

*²But Abram said, "O L*ORD GOD, *what will you give me, for I continue childless, and the heir of my house is Eliezer of Damascus?"*

³And Abram said, "Behold, you have given me no offspring, and a member of my household will be my heir."

*⁴And behold, the word of the L*ORD *came to him: "This man shall not be your heir; your very own son shall be your heir."*

⁵And he brought him outside and said, "Look toward heaven, and number the stars, if you are able to number them." Then he said to him, "So shall your offspring be."

*⁶And he believed the L*ORD, *and he counted it to him as righteousness.*

- What does the imagery of God being a shield mean to you?

Genesis 15 is a high point in the story of Abraham and Sarah, and in redemptive history. Here, in dramatic splendor, God explains His lavish, persevering, undeserved, unconditional love for His chosen ones as He introduces into human history the doctrine of justification. John Calvin called justification "the main hinge on which religion turns".[2] The word justification is not used, but verse 6 is quoted in the New Testament in connection with justification.

For if Abraham was justified by works, he has something to boast about, but not before God. For what does the Scripture say? "Abraham believed God, and it was counted to him as righteousness." Now to the one who works, his wages are not counted as a gift but as his due. And to the one who does not work but trusts him who justifies the ungodly, his faith is counted as righteousness (Rom. 4:2-5; see also Rom. 4:22; Gal. 3:6; James 2:23).

For such a great doctrine, we defer to some of the great theologians of the past and present.

James Boice: "Justification by faith is God's answer to the most basic of all religious questions, namely, how can a man or woman become right with God? ... The doctrine of justification by faith is the most important of all Christian doctrines because it tells how one who is in rebellion against God may become right with him. It says that we may be justified, not by our own works-righteousness, but solely by the work of Christ received by faith."[3]

Martin Luther: "When the article of justification has fallen, everything has fallen ... This is the chief article from which all other doctrines have flowed ... It alone begets, nourishes, builds, preserves, and defends the church of God; and without it the church of God cannot exist for one hour."[4]

Westminster Shorter Catechism: "Justification is an act of God's free grace, wherein he pardoneth all our sins, and accepteth us as righteous in his sight only for the righteousness of Christ imputed to us, and received by faith alone."[5]

J. V. Fesko: [Gen. 15:6] "is like a lightning bolt flashing in a small, dark room. First, Abraham believed, placing his faith in the Lord's promise, what Paul calls the gospel. Second, God looked upon Abraham, not as a condemned sinner, but as a righteous man. In terms of the greater testimony of the rest of Scripture, righteousness is something that a person can only achieve through complete and perfect obedience to the entire law of God (Lev. 18:5; Deut. 27-30; Gal. 3:10-14; Rom. 10:5). Yet, Abraham received this righteous status by looking through faith to the promise of God. Third ... God 'counted' Abraham's belief as righteousness ... To count, credit, or impute righteousness to a person means that this righteousness is alien; it is not native to Abraham ... From where did this righteousness come? It was to come from God himself, God in the flesh, the promised seed of the woman, the seed of Abraham."[6]

This is not just theological jargon. This is family history. Paul quotes Genesis 15:6 and then unflinchingly identifies Abraham's family: "... it is those of faith who are sons of Abraham" (Gal. 3:7).

Justification is an *act* — a one-time declaration by God of the change He makes in our status. Then He begins to make us in *practice* what we are in position. He sanctifies us. "Sanctification is the work of God's free grace, whereby we are renewed in the whole man after the image of God, and are enabled more and more to die unto sin, and live unto righteousness."[7]

Sanctification is a life-long process of growing in the grace and knowledge of Jesus that culminates in glorification when, at death, Christians are "made perfect in holiness, and do immediately pass into glory ... "[8]

In justification and glorification, we are passive. In sanctification, the Holy Spirit motivates and empowers us to trust and obey. As we grow in our knowledge of the Person, plan, and purpose of God, our character and desires are gradually transformed and we increasingly integrate the gospel into all of life. *Knowing* is so very important, so after learning that the righteousness of the Promised One was credited to his account, Abraham asked a transformative question.

> [7]And he said to him, "I am the LORD who brought you out from Ur of the Chaldeans to give you this land to possess."

> [8]But he said, "O LORD GOD, how am I to know that I shall possess it?"

Abraham's statement of faith precedes his question. He refers to God as *Yahweh*, the personal God of covenant faithfulness, and as *Elohim*, the sovereign Creator. What happens next seems peculiar, but it is a precious illustration of justification by grace alone. It is God's answer to the "how can I know" question.

> [9]He said to him, "Bring me a heifer three years old, a female goat three years old, a ram three years old, a turtledove, and a young pigeon."

> [10]And he brought him all these, cut them in half, and laid each half over against the other. But he did not cut the birds in half.

[11]And when birds of prey came down on the carcasses, Abram drove them away.

[12]As the sun was going down, a deep sleep fell on Abram. And behold, dreadful and great darkness fell upon him.

[13]Then the LORD said to Abram, "Know for certain that your offspring will be sojourners in a land that is not theirs and will be servants there, and they will be afflicted for four hundred years.

[14]But I will bring judgment on the nation that they serve, and afterward they shall come out with great possessions.

[15]As for yourself, you shall go to your fathers in peace; you shall be buried in a good old age.

[16]And they shall come back here in the fourth generation, for the iniquity of the Amorites is not yet complete."

[17]When the sun had gone down and it was dark, behold, a smoking fire pot and a flaming torch passed between these pieces.

[18]On that day the LORD made a covenant with Abram, saying, "To your offspring I give this land ..."

God's answer to Abraham's question is a magnificent preview of Christ our Savior.

LIVING COVENANTALLY

I therefore, a prisoner for the Lord, urge you to walk in a manner worthy of the calling to which you have been called, with all humility and gentleness, with patience, bearing with one another in love, eager to maintain the unity of the Spirit in the bond of peace.

(Eph. 4:1-3)

How can I Know? Genesis 15:8-21

By bearing the full consequences of the covenantal pledge to death, Christ delivered us from the curse of our inability to live up to the covenant so that we might become heirs of its blessings.[9]
Nancy Guthrie

How many times had Abraham and Sarah discussed the question he now asks in Genesis 15:8? Even after we are justified, there are times when we ask:

- How can I know your promises are true?
- How can I know all things will work together for good when things are so bad?
- How can I know you love me after what I have done?
- How can I know you are with me when I am so lonely?
- How can I know you will never leave me when I have been abandoned by one I love?
- How can I know there is a heaven and I will go there?

God answers the "how can I know" question by cutting a covenant. This was a common ritual in antiquity when two people made a covenant. They walked between the pieces of slaughtered animals, legally binding them to keep certain promises and signifying a self-curse if they did not; they would suffer the fate of the dead animals. But Abraham did not walk the bloody path. He was asleep, a deep sleep, totally passive. The "dreadful and great darkness" points to the scandal at Calvary when "there was darkness over the whole land until the ninth hour, while the sun's light failed ..." (Luke 23:44-45). When the smoking fire pot and flaming torch, representing God's Presence, passed through the pieces of slain animals, God was promising that if the covenant was broken, He alone would bear the penalty.

Jesus, the Righteous One, walked the bloody path, not because God broke covenant but because we did. When Jesus hung on the cross, He bore the full curse of the Father's wrath against our sin. Jesus was torn from His Father so we never will be, for all eternity. Not only did He pay our debt, He filled our account with His righteousness. And all the while we slept, oblivious to the death He died in our place. We can add nothing to what He did.

> God shows his love for us in that while we were still sinners, Christ died for us. Since, therefore, we have now been justified by his blood, much more shall we be saved by him from the wrath of God. (Rom. 5:8-9)

This covenant is initiated, administered and kept by God. Grace, grace and more grace.

So when we wonder, "How can I know?" we look to the Cross, and we know.

Imagine Abraham throwing back the tent door and shouting to Sarah, "Now I know how we know!" The Abrahamic covenant was not just cerebral for them. There was dancing in the tent that night.

*P*oints to *P*onder

Does your heart dance as you meditate on the doctrine of justification by grace alone?

How do you feel knowing that your sin-debt has been paid in full?

How do you feel knowing that the Righteousness of the Perfect One has been put in your bank account?

Have you had a "how can I know" moment?

How did it help you know more of God's love in Christ for you?

Transformed by Prayer

When my soul was embittered ...

I was like a beast toward you.

Nevertheless, I am continually with you;

you hold my right hand.

You guide me with your counsel,

and afterward you will receive me to glory.

Whom have I in heaven but you?

And there is nothing on earth that I desire besides you.
                                                    (Ps. 73:21-25)

Echoes of Eden: Genesis 16:1-6

The gospel of justifying faith means ... that we are more wicked than we ever dared believe, but more loved and accepted in Christ than we ever dared hope–at the very same time.[10]

Tim Keller

We *know*, but we forget so quickly. Sarah believed the promise, but as she stood at the fork in the road, she *acted* within the limits of her experience and abilities.

Now Sarai, Abram's wife, had borne him no children. She had a female Egyptian servant whose name was Hagar. And Sarai said to Abram, "Behold now, the LORD has prevented me from bearing children. Go in to my servant; it may be that I shall obtain children by her ..." (Gen. 16:1-2)

This was a common practice in ancient times; however, just because something is culturally accepted does not mean it is right. Sarah's decision to help God echoes Eve's attitude after the birth of Cain: "I've gotten a man with the help of the LORD" (Gen. 4:1). We are wired to be helpers. When there is a problem, our helper instincts go into action. But the helper design runs amok when we fret about the crisis rather than trusting God's sovereignty. The beauty and strength of our design becomes horribly twisted when we scheme, manipulate and control in order to "help God" move things along.

"And Abram listened to the voice of Sarai" (Gen. 16:2). Abraham and Sarah trusted self. Their actions were disconnected from their declaration of faith in God's promise.

Another echo — Adam listened to Eve, and we know how that turned out. Every woman should prayerfully consider the power of her words. Are they life-taking or life-giving?

So, after Abram had lived ten years in the land of Canaan, Sarai, Abram's wife, took Hagar the Egyptian, her servant, and gave her to Abram her husband as a wife. And he went in to Hagar, and she conceived. And when she saw that she had conceived, she looked with contempt on her mistress. And Sarai said to Abram, "May the wrong done to me be on you! I gave my servant to your embrace, and when she saw that she had conceived, she looked on me with contempt. May the LORD judge between you and me!" But Abram said to Sarai, "Behold, your servant is in your power; do to her as you please." Then Sarai dealt harshly with her, and she fled from her. (Gen 16:3-6)

The raw reality of Sarah's solution feels uncomfortably familiar. Hagar became arrogant and turned on Sarah. The rivalry was ugly. Sarah was furious and blamed Abraham. He threw up his hands and said, "Do whatever you please." And Sarah dealt harshly with Hagar.

News-flash: Our situation and relationships do not *make* us manipulative and harsh. They *reveal* the wickedness in our hearts.

Sarah had grown in her knowledge of God, so did she now see herself in light of His goodness? Did her harshness shock her? Did she grieve over her sin? Did she repent? Do I when my wickedness goes public?

As we know God and know ourselves, we increasingly know that "we are more wicked than we ever dared believe, but more loved and accepted in Christ than we ever dared hope — at the very same time." This gospel of justifying faith is transformative.

Points to Ponder

Have you dared to face your wickedness?

Have you dared to believe that God loves and accepts you in Christ?

How are you showing His love and acceptance to others?

Transformed by Prayer

Hear, O LORD, when I cry aloud;

be gracious to me and answer me!

You have said, "Seek my face."

My heart says to you,

"Your face, LORD, do I seek."

Hide not your face from me.

Turn not your servant away in anger,

O you who have been my help ...

Teach me your way, O LORD,

and lead me on a level path.

(Ps. 27:7-9, 11)

Life-taking Losses: Genesis 16:7-16

Much of the impotence of American churches is tied to a profound ignorance and apathy about justification. Our people live in a fog of guilt. Or just as bad, they think being a better person is all God requires.[11]

Kevin DeYoung

The wrong road looks right because "The heart is deceitful above all things, and desperately sick ... " (Jer. 17:9). It seemed innocent and life-giving. Beautiful fruit to make one wise. A woman to birth a child. So Eve gave the fruit to her husband and Sarah gave Hagar to her husband. Eve and Sarah trusted self and their life-taking actions led to horrendous losses.

Adam and Eve lost paradise. Sarah lost respect for her husband and reverence for God as her barrenness turned to bitterness. Hagar lost her home and hope of living. Abraham lost his only son and one of his wives. So where is hope in the midst of this hurt?

The angel of the LORD found her [Hagar] by a spring of water in the wilderness, the spring on the way to Shur. And he said, "Hagar, servant of Sarai, where have you come from and where are you going?" She said, "I am fleeing from my mistress Sarai." The angel of the LORD said to her, "Return to your mistress and submit to her." The angel of the LORD also said to her, "I will surely multiply your offspring so that they cannot be numbered for multitude." And the angel of the LORD said to her,

"Behold, you are pregnant and shall bear a son.
You shall call his name Ishmael,
because the LORD has listened to your affliction.
He shall be a wild donkey of a man,
his hand against everyone
and everyone's hand against him,
and he shall dwell over against all his kinsmen."

So she called the name of the LORD who spoke to her, "You are a God of seeing," for she said, "Truly here I have seen him who

looks after me." Therefore the well was called Beer-lahai-roi ...
(Gen. 16:7-14)

As Hagar runs toward Shur, her Egyptian home, an angel finds her at an oasis in a barren desert. He asks the questions every elect exile needs to answer: "Where have you come from and where are you going?" The imperative to return and relinquish (submit) was followed by the promise of God's presence and provision. She responds by calling God *El Roi* –"I have seen the one who sees me"– and calling the place *Beer-lahai-roi* –"well of the Living One who sees me".

Sarah's solution sucked the life out of the people in her home and produced Ishmael, a wild donkey of a man. There were ongoing consequences of Sarah's actions, but God did not deal harshly with her because He loved her. His command to Hagar to return and relinquish is full of mercy because it shows straying pilgrims the way back. It is a potent picture of repentance. Hagar's daily presence would confront Sarah with her need to repent and to drink deeply from the well of the Living One, to taste His loving-kindness (*hesed*) until gradually *hesed* replaced harshness in her heart. When we do this, our loss (self) becomes our gain (Jesus).

Has there been a time when your heart deceived you and your actions were life-taking?

How did drinking from the well of the Living One who sees you transform you?

Do you need to drink from that well right now?

Transformed by Prayer

In you, O LORD, do I take refuge;

let me never be put to shame!

In your righteousness deliver me and rescue me;

incline your ear to me, and save me!

Be to me a rock of refuge,

to which I may continually come;

you have given the command to save me,

for you are my rock and my fortress. (Ps. 71:1-3)

What's In A Name: Genesis 17:1-7

Justification is the very hinge and pillar of Christianity. An error about justification is dangerous, like a defect in a foundation.[12]

Thomas Watson

In Scripture names are instructive.

When Abram was ninety-nine years old the LORD appeared to Abram and said to him, "I am God Almighty; walk before me, and be blameless, that I may make my covenant between me and you, and may multiply you greatly." (Gen. 17:1-2)

The imperative to "be blameless" is preceded by God's revelation of Himself as God Almighty – *El Shaddai.*

El points to the fact that God is the sovereign, almighty, powerful one. *Shad* means breast and points to God's fullness and bounty, His tenderness, generosity and nurture. In this name, the greatness of His power and the gentleness of His care coalesce. This name is especially meaningful for women because it poignantly pictures our life-giving calling to be spiritual mothers. He alone is the one who gives us the capacity to fulfill this mission to be fruitful and multiply.

Then Abram fell on his face. (Gen.17:3)

This is how sanctification works. The more we know God as He reveals Himself in His Word, the more we fall before Him in wonder and worship because the blamelessness of Christ has been credited to us. Note what *El Shaddai* says *He will do.*

... And God said to him, "Behold, my covenant is with you, and you shall be the father of a multitude of nations. No longer shall your name be called Abram, but your name shall be Abraham for I have made you the father of a multitude of nations. I will make you exceedingly fruitful, and I will make you into nations, and kings shall come from you. And I will establish my covenant between me and you and your offspring after you throughout their generations for an everlasting covenant, to be God to you and to your offspring after you." (Gen. 17:3-7)

Abram means "high father" and Abraham means "father of a multitude". Later God changes Sarai, meaning "my princess" to Sarah, which means "mother of nations". Abram and Sarai are names that point backward. Abraham and Sarah are names that point forward to the promise. Their new names highlight God's power as the ultimate Life-Giver. They are told to name their son Isaac, meaning "laughter", as a reminder that God answered their laughter with the joy of a covenant blessing.

Abraham and Sarah are our spiritual father and mother because in Christ we are numbered among their offspring. Our names are changed from orphan, alien, stranger to beloved daughter and we, too, can be a spiritual mother to many.

God tells Abraham amazing things that He will *do*, but tucked into this passage is a precious promise of what He will *be* to him; "I will be God to you and to your offspring after you" (Gen 17:7). This is the essence of the covenant of grace. God binds Himself to us in Christ in an unbreakable bond. Our relationship with God does not begin with *us* choosing God to be our God; it begins with *God* choosing to be our God.

Points to Ponder

What is your response to the name El Shaddai?

What difference does God's unbreakable promise make in your life?

Have you ever thought of your potential to be a spiritual mother to many?

Transformed by Prayer

O God, save me, by your name,

and vindicate me by your might.

O God, hear my prayer;

give ear to the words of my mouth.

With a freewill offering I will sacrifice to you;

I will give thanks to your name, O Lord, *for it is good.*

(Ps. 54:1, 2, 6)

Worth the Wait: Genesis 17

The Lord is good to those who wait for him, to the soul who seeks him. It is good that one should wait quietly for the salvation of the Lord.

(Lam. 3:25-26)

Waiting is hard, but so sanctifying. Abraham and Sarah waited twenty-four years. And then, for the first time, God makes it absolutely clear that Sarah will be the mother of God's set-apart people.

And God said to Abraham, "As for Sarai your wife, you shall not call her name Sarai, but Sarah shall be her name. I will bless her, and moreover, I will give you a son by her. I will bless her, and she shall become nations; kings of peoples shall come from her".
(Gen. 17:15-16)

Abraham's response is understandable.

Then Abraham fell on his face and laughed and said to himself, "Shall a child be born to a man who is a hundred years old? Shall Sarah, who is ninety years old, bear a child?" And Abraham said to God, "Oh that Ishmael might live before you!" God said, "No, but Sarah your wife shall bear you a son, and you shall call his name Isaac. I will establish my covenant with him as an everlasting covenant for his offspring after him". (Gen 17:17-19)

Life would come from a dead womb. This is grace. Unexpected. Undeserved. Unrelenting.

[Abraham] did not weaken in faith when he considered his own body, which was as good as dead (since he was about a hundred years old), or when he considered the barrenness of Sarah's womb. No unbelief made him waver concerning the promise of God, but he grew strong in his faith as he gave glory to God, fully convinced that God was able to do what he had promised.
(Rom. 4:19-21)

Imagine Abraham trying to convince Sarah that she was going to carry a baby in her womb. My response would be, "Crazy old man". We'll see how Sarah responded next.

Points to Ponder

Why is waiting on the Lord so hard?

How is it life-taking when we do not wait patiently for the Lord?

How does it help you wait well when you remember that "according to his promise we are waiting for new heavens and a new earth in which righteousness dwells"? (2 Pet. 3:13)

Transformed by Prayer

Out of the depths I cry to you, O LORD!

> *O LORD, hear my voice!*

Let your ears be attentive

> *to the voice of my pleas for mercy!*

If you, O LORD, should mark iniquities,

> *O LORD, who could stand?*

But with you there is forgiveness,

> *that you may be feared.*

I wait for the LORD, my soul waits,

> *and in his word I hope;*

my soul waits for the LORD

> *more than watchmen for the morning,*
>
> *more than watchmen for the morning.*

(Ps. 130:1-6)

SEVEN

Sarah's Son

Genesis 18–23

CINDY'S STORY

Cindy Hennessy, from Naperville, Illinois, is a wife, mother, and CiCi (grandmother).

As a small girl I sang *Jesus Loves Me* to my dog, but it was not until I was in my mid-thirties that I understood and believed it. I was newly married in a blended family with three small children. As I began to dig deeper into my new faith, I realized how little I knew about living a God-honoring life. My selfishness surfaced as I realized I was doing the right things for the wrong reasons. As I attended Bible studies and became involved in church, God was teaching me to trust Him, but I was in a state of turmoil, being pulled between my old life and this new life.

Our oldest son, Jack, joined the Army just prior to 9/11 and served during the Iraq War. While Jack was overseas, I was ministering to a woman with a terminal illness. Knowing that death was possible for one and imminent for the other, I began to wonder how I would cope. I could not fix either situation. I remember thinking, "If Jack dies, will I still believe? Where will my strength come from?"

In the hours after learning the tragic news of Jack's death, a deep and heavy sorrow, along with a peace that belies description, enveloped our home and our lives. It was a time of transformation for me. I had to rely on God and His Word. Nothing from the world or within me had the power to help. I had to trust God with this woman's life and Jack's absence.

It has been eleven years since Jack's death. Through grief, I have come to understand the joy in the suffering. The joy is His transforming power that continues to change me into the life-giving woman he created me to be. My marriage, relationships and heart are full of life; His Loving Life.

THINKING BIBLICALLY

The New Testament is in the Old concealed; The Old Testament is in the New revealed.

Augustine

Genesis 18

¹*And the LORD appeared to him by the oaks of Mamre, as he sat at the door of his tent in the heat of the day.*

²*He lifted up his eyes and looked, and behold, three men were standing in front of him. When he saw them, he ran from the tent door to meet them and bowed himself to the earth*

³*and said, "O Lord, if I have found favor in your sight, do not pass by your servant.*

⁴*Let a little water be brought, and wash your feet, and rest yourselves under the tree,*

⁵*while I bring a morsel of bread, that you may refresh yourselves, and after that you may pass on—since you have come to your servant." So they said, "Do as you have said."*

⁶*And Abraham went quickly into the tent to Sarah and said, "Quick! Three seahs of fine flour! Knead it, and make cakes."*

⁷*And Abraham ran to the herd and took a calf, tender and good, and gave it to a young man, who prepared it quickly.*

⁸*Then he took curds and milk and the calf that he had prepared, and set it before them. And he stood by them under the tree while they ate.*

Was the writer of Hebrews thinking of this scene when he wrote: "Do not neglect to show hospitality to strangers, for thereby some have entertained angels unawares" (13:2)? As Sarah launched into a tornado of tasks it is unlikely that she realized their story was about to crescendo. In Genesis 18-22 we will finally understand why Peter refers to Sarah as the mother of those who "do good and do not fear anything that is frightening" (1 Pet. 3:6).

⁹*They said to him, "Where is Sarah your wife?" And he said, "She is in the tent."*

- What promise did God make in Genesis 17:15-16?

It is doubtful that Abraham could convince Sarah she would be the biological mother of the promised child, but he didn't need to. In tender mercy, the Lord appears at Abraham's tent. He knew Sarah would hear His next words.

> [10]*The LORD said, "I will surely return to you about this time next year, and Sarah your wife shall have a son." And Sarah was listening at the tent door behind him.*

> [11]*Now Abraham and Sarah were old, advanced in years. The way of women had ceased to be with Sarah.*

- How old were Abraham and Sarah? (see Gen. 17:17)

- What would you have thought if you had been listening?

> [12]*So Sarah laughed to herself, saying, "After I am worn out, and my lord is old, shall I have pleasure?"*

> [13]*The LORD said to Abraham, "Why did Sarah laugh and say, 'Shall I indeed bear a child, now that I am old?'*

- Underline Sarah's "I" statements in Genesis 18:12-13.

- Why do you think Sarah laughed?

God speaks and Sarah laughs. Just like Eve, Sarah has an "I" orientation. God's question strikes at the heart of bifurcated faith. Sarah knows the information but does not pursue transformation. God knows her thoughts and He pursues her.

> [14]*Is anything too hard for the Lord? At the appointed time I will return to you about this time next year, and Sarah shall have a son."*

> [15]*But Sarah denied it, saying, "I did not laugh," for she was afraid. He said, "No, but you did laugh."*

- Underline the Lord's question in Genesis 18:14.

- Underline His "I will" promise.

- What difference does the question and the promise make when you stand at the fork in the road?

"Is anything too hard for the Lord?" is the determinative question for Sarah and for us. This is not about Sarah's power to conceive. This is about God's power to do the impossible.

His promise to return is a foretaste of what is to come. Jesus said, "And if I go and prepare a place for you, I will come again and will take you to myself, that where I am you may be also" (John 14:3).

Then, before the Lord's return, there was the trip to the Gerar.

Genesis 20

> [1] From there Abraham journeyed toward the territory of the Negeb and lived between Kadesh and Shur; and he sojourned in Gerar.

> [2] And Abraham said of Sarah his wife, "She is my sister." And Abimelech king of Gerar sent and took Sarah.

We don't know why they went, but when they got there it was a replay of their trip to Egypt almost twenty-five years earlier (Gen. 12:10-20). Chronic sin keeps popping up. So does God's grace.

> [3] But God came to Abimelech in a dream by night and said to him, "Behold, you are a dead man because of the woman whom you have taken, for she is a man's wife."

> [4] Now Abimelech had not approached her. So he said, "Lord, will you kill an innocent people?

> [5] Did he not himself say to me, 'She is my sister'? And she herself said, 'He is my brother.' In the integrity of my heart and the innocence of my hands I have done this."

> [6] Then God said to him in the dream, "Yes, I know that you have done this in the integrity of your heart, and it was I who kept you from sinning against me. Therefore I did not let you touch her.

• Why had Abimelech not approached Sarah?

"It was I who kept you from sinning against me" (Gen. 20:6). The sovereignty of God is stunning. The love of God is lavish. When we are in Christ, our identity with Him is so complete that when someone sins against us, they sin against Him.

7Now then, return the man's wife, for he is a prophet, so that he will pray for you, and you shall live. But if you do not return her, know that you shall surely die, you, and all who are yours."

- How does God define Abraham?

Instead of condemning Abraham, God refers to him as a prophet. "There is therefore now no condemnation for those who are in Christ Jesus" (Rom. 8:1). His identification with us is not based on our performance but on the perfect performance of Jesus for us; however, He does not ignore our sin. He reveals our sin patterns, gives us repenting grace, and restores us to redemptive ministry. Thus shall it be until Jesus returns.

LIVING COVENANTALLY

We are God's people, the chosen of the Lord,
Born of his Spirit, established by his Word;
Our cornerstone is Christ alone, and strong in him we stand:
O let us live transparently, and walk heart to heart and hand in hand.[1]
Bryan Jeffery Leech

Immeasurably More: Genesis 18:1-15

Oh, the blessed restfulness of putting everything–physical, mental, and spiritual–into my Father's hands, and just leaving all there! When once faith can heartily make this transfer, all is well with the soul, and its peace is perfect.[2]

Susannah Spurgeon

Sarah was never able to produce a child through her own efforts. Her barrenness needed divine intervention. She needed a visit from *Yahweh*, the God of covenant love and loyalty, who is able to do immeasurably more than anything we can imagine. She heard His promise, but her perceived circumstances trumped the covenant promise. She tried to cover her unbelief with a ridiculous lie, "I did not laugh". It was time for Sarah to just be quiet. It was time to "Be still, and know that I am God" (Ps. 46:10). Knowing the transforming truth, "I am God", is impossible for us, but not for God.

> *I will set my eyes on them for good ...* **I will give them a heart to know that I am the** Lord, *and they shall be my people and I will be their God, for they shall return to me with their whole heart.* (Jer. 24:6-7)

God showed Sarah the truth about herself and about Him. He transformed her from faith in her own strategies to deeper faith in His power to do what He promised, without her help. And, as always, His word accomplished its purpose.

> *By faith Sarah herself received power to conceive, even when she was past the age, since she considered him faithful who had promised.* (Heb. 11:11)

God's "immeasurably more" put faith in Sarah's doubting heart and life in her dead womb. An exquisite picture of becoming a life-giver. Her story shows God's tenacious love in proving to us that He "is able to do immeasurably more than anything we can imagine, according to his power that is at work within us" (Eph. 3:20 NIV).

So let's join Paul in his prayer that we will "know the love of Christ that surpasses knowledge, that [we] may be filled with all the fullness of God" (Eph. 3:19).

$\mathcal{P}$oints to $\mathcal{P}$onder

In the midst of the noise and clutter of your life are you learning to be still and know that He is God?

Are you waiting for those immeasurably-more moments rather than fretting and strategizing to "fix" everything and everybody?

Transformed by Prayer

I bow my knees before the Father ... And I pray that you, being rooted and established in love, may have power, together with all the saints, to grasp how wide and long and high and deep is the love of Christ, and to know this love that surpasses knowledge—that you may be filled to the measure of all the fullness of God. Now to him who is able to do immeasurably more than all that we ask or imagine, according to his power that is at work within us, to him be glory in the church and in Christ Jesus throughout all generations, forever and ever. Amen.

(Eph. 3:14-21, NIV)

The Master's Masterpiece : Genesis 19:1-26

When we pray that our lives may glorify Him, we are asking that the self may be put down ... We must be prepared to lose ourselves ... Losing an argument for His sake, losing something we held dear, losing face, reputation, a position of power or superiority, losing a claim on someone or on his affection or respect—can these be a part of the answer to our prayer to glorify God in our lives? Assuredly they can, for assuredly the Son Himself laid aside all such assets when He came to do the will of the Father.[3]

Elisabeth Elliot

It was a busy year. A lot happened between God's promise that Sarah would be a mother (Gen. 18:10), and before "the LORD visited Sarah" (Gen. 21:1). In addition to the trip to Gerar, there was Sodom.

God tells Abraham He will destroy Sodom and Gomorrah. Abraham intercedes, and God sends angels to rescue Abraham's nephew, Lot, and his family.

*... the angels urged Lot, saying, "Up! Take your wife and your two daughters who are here, lest you be swept away in the punishment of the city." But he lingered. So the men seized him and his wife and his two daughters by the hand, **the LORD being merciful to him,** and they brought him out ... "Escape for your life. Do not look back" ... Then the LORD rained on Sodom and Gomorrah sulfur and fire ... But Lot's wife, behind him, looked back, and she became a pillar of salt. (Gen. 19:15-17, 24, 26)*

We don't know much about Mrs. Lot, but we do know God's Word was not her authority.

The Hebrew word translated "pillar" in this passage means to be stopped and trapped in a still position. Life-takers are trapped in static, self-centered immaturity. Jesus gives a chilling warning.

Likewise, just as it was in the days of Lot—they were eating and drinking, buying and selling, planting and building, but on the day when Lot went out from Sodom, fire and sulfur rained from heaven and destroyed them all—so will it be on the day when the Son of Man is revealed ... Remember Lot's wife. Whoever seeks to preserve his life will lose it, but whoever loses his life will keep it. (Luke 17:28-30, 32-33)

Mrs. Lot lost everything. But "the Lord being merciful" provides a way of escape (1 Cor. 10:13). We don't have to become pillars of salt. God gives a striking contrast to this imagery in Psalm 144:12:

May our ... daughters [be] like corner pillars cut for the structure of a palace.

This Hebrew word translated "pillar" refers to a functional, supportive, often beautifully carved pillar that gives stability and beauty to a structure. The word translated "cut" refers to striking wood or marble to shape, smooth and carve it.

Striking, shaping, and smoothing is a tedious, tender, transforming process.

The Lord God sovereignly chooses hearts of stone and replaces them with hearts of flesh (Ezek. 11:19). He slowly carves them into supportive pillars that give gospel beauty and strength to relationships and situations.

We are His workmanship and our Sovereign Sculptor will not stop working on His Masterpiece.

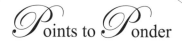

Points to Ponder

How are you being carved right now?

*Are you resisting or yielding to your Sculptor's striking,
shaping and smoothing to form "the hidden person
of the heart with the imperishable beauty of
a gentle and quiet spirit, which in God's sight
is very precious"? (1 Pet. 3:4)*

Transformed by Prayer

Incline your ear, O LORD, and answer me,

for I am poor and needy ...

For you, O LORD, are good and forgiving,

abounding in steadfast love to all who call upon you.

Give ear, O LORD, to my prayer;

listen to my plea for grace ...

For you are great and do wondrous things;

you alone are God.

(Ps. 86:1, 5-6, 10)

Who Is Your Mother? Genesis 21

*God is our aim. The fight of faith against wrong thinking is
the fight to stay satisfied with God. Whether it's bad thoughts,
daydreams, questionable behavior, or what transpires on a Friday
night date, the fight of faith is always to stay satisfied with God
... And what whets our appetite for maximum joy in the Lord?
You guessed it—God's Word. The role of the Word of God is to
feed faith's appetite for Jesus Christ.[4]*

Joni Eareckson Tada

After twenty-five years of waiting, it happened.

*The LORD visited Sarah as he had said, and the LORD did
to Sarah as he had promised. And Sarah conceived and bore
Abraham a son in his old age at the time of which God had
spoken to him. (Gen. 21:1-2)*

Abraham named his son Isaac as God had commanded
(Gen. 17:19). Isaac means laughter. Soon the joyful laughter was
confronted with scornful laughter.

*And the child grew and was weaned. And Abraham made a great
feast on the day that Isaac was weaned. But Sarah saw the
son of Hagar the Egyptian, whom she had borne to Abraham,
laughing. So she said to Abraham, "Cast out this slave woman
with her son, for the son of this slave woman shall not be heir
with my son Isaac." And the thing was very displeasing to
Abraham on account of his son. But God said to Abraham,
"Be not displeased because of the boy and because of your slave
woman. Whatever Sarah says to you, do as she tells you, for
through Isaac shall your offspring be named". (Gen.21:8-12)*

Is Sarah over-reacting? Is she still dealing harshly with Hagar?
The *Spirit of the Reformation Study Bible* explains:

Sarah perceived the significance of Ishmael's disdain
for Isaac and his threat to her son's inheritance ... The
Hebrew ... form [for laughter] here signifies "to laugh
malevolently." The son of the slave woman persecuted the
son of the free woman (see Gal. 4:29).[5]

This is more than a rivalry between two women. Paul uses this as an allegory to show the contrast between grace and works. In his study on Galatians, Tim Keller writes, "Hagar represents being saved by works while Isaac and Sarah represent being saved by grace" (see Gal. 4:21-31).

Grace and works must not be mingled. Sarah's previous schemes and strategies to help God keep His promises were life-taking. As she looks at Isaac, the life conceived in her dead womb, she finally knows, nothing is impossible with God. His grace is sufficient. His grace must not be compromised. We are justified and sanctified by grace alone through faith alone in Christ alone.

Abraham is the spiritual father of the heirs of the promise, but he is also the father of Ishmael's descendants. The question is: Who is your mother, Hagar or Sarah? Do you trust your good works or Christ alone?

> Listen to me, you who pursue righteousness,
> you who seek the LORD:
> look to the rock from which you were hewn,
> and to the quarry from which you were dug.
> Look to Abraham your father and to Sarah who bore you ...
> (Isa. 51:1-2).

Sarah took a risk. What if Abraham chose Hagar and Ishmael? Apparently faith overcame fear because the inheritance, the gospel, was at stake. Fearless women who are saved by grace do gospel-good in the power of that grace. Daughters of Sarah refuse to compromise the gospel in order to accommodate cultural morals. They choose life even when it is an unplanned and inconvenient pregnancy. They extend forgiveness to those who hurt them. They "do good and do not fear anything that is frightening" (1 Pet. 3:6).

Points to *Ponder*

Are you pursuing righteousness in order to earn more of God's love? This is works-righteousness.

Pray for grace to be motivated and empowered by God's unconditional love to pursue righteousness for His glory.

Transformed by Prayer

Your righteousness, O God,

reaches the high heavens.

You who have done great things,

O God, who is like you? ...

I will also praise you with the harp

for your faithfulness, O my God ...

My lips will shout for joy,

when I sing praises to you;

my soul also, which you have redeemed.

And my tongue will talk of your righteous help all the day long ...

(Ps. 71:19, 22-24)

The Lord Provides: Genesis 22

More love to Thee, O Christ, more love to Thee!
Hear thou the prayer I make on bended knee;
This is my earnest plea, more love, O Christ to Thee,
More love to Thee, more love to Thee![6]

Elizabeth Prentiss

This familiar chapter is crammed with pointers to the gospel.

After these things God tested Abraham and said to him, "Abraham!" And he said, "Here I am." He said, "Take your son, your only son Isaac, whom you love, and go to the land of Moriah, and offer him there as a burnt offering ..." (Gen. 22:1-2)

Abraham's "here I am" is an open-hearted, open-handed response. The command defies reason. Isaac was the son of promise. How would God keep the promise if Abraham obeyed? This summons will lead him to walk by faith and not by sight, to choose the Giver rather than the gift. We cannot imagine how this command pierced Abraham's heart. As we look beyond Abraham, we see the heart of our Father "who did not spare his own Son but gave him up for us all" (Rom. 8:32).

Moriah is the place where Solomon built the temple (2 Chron. 3:1). It is the area where Jesus was crucified.

So Abraham rose early in the morning ... and went to the place of which God had told him. (Gen. 22:3)

This time, when the road divides there is no hesitation. Abraham's immediate obedience indicates that obeying God had become a settled issue for him. He acted on the basis of his knowledge of God (Heb. 11:17-19).

On the third day Abraham lifted up his eyes and saw the place from afar. Then Abraham said to his young men, "Stay here with the donkey; I and the boy will go over there and worship and come again to you." (Gen. 22:4-5)

The third day would be a day of reversal and redemption.

*And Abraham took the wood of the burnt offering and laid it
on Isaac his son. And he took in his hand the fire and the knife.
So they went both of them together. And Isaac said to his father
Abraham, "My father! ... Behold, the fire and the wood, but
where is the lamb for a burnt offering?" Abraham said, "God
will provide for himself the lamb for a burnt offering, my son."
... Abraham built the altar there and laid the wood in order and
bound Isaac his son and laid him on the altar, on top of the
wood. Then Abraham reached out his hand and took the knife
to slaughter his son.* (Gen. 22:6-10)

This was a journey and a mission between a father and his son.
Lean forward. See Jesus carrying His cross to Moriah. See the Father
holding the fire and the knife, symbols of judgment. No Roman
soldier could put Jesus on the cross against His will. No emperor
could kill Him. Calvary was a Divine transaction when the Father
laid the sin of His people on His sinless Son, and the Son endured
the fire and judgment of the Father's wrath against sin.

The angel of the Lord called to Abraham and told him not
to lay his hand on Isaac.

*And Abraham lifted up his eyes and looked, and behold, behind
him was a ram, caught in a thicket by his horns. And Abraham
went and took the ram and offered it up as a burnt offering
instead of his son. So Abraham called the name of that place,
"The LORD will provide"; as it is said to this day, "On the mount
of the LORD it shall be provided."* (Gen. 22:13-14)

Abraham calls the place *Jehovah Jireh*, "the LORD will provide". As
he rejoices in God's present grace, He proclaims future grace by
pointing to the Substitute God "will provide" for His people. God
stops Abraham, but God did not stop when His Son was on the
altar, "His wrath [was] poured out like fire" (Nahum 1:6). "Since,
therefore, we have now been justified by his blood, much more
shall we be saved by him from the wrath of God" (Rom. 5:9).

*And the angel of the LORD called to Abraham a second time
from heaven and said "... I will surely bless you, and I will surely
multiply your offspring as the stars of heaven and as the sand that
is on the seashore. And your offspring shall possess the gate of his*

enemies, and in your offspring shall all the nations of the earth be blessed, because you have obeyed my voice." (Gen. 22:15, 17-18)

The Offspring is Jesus, "And if you are Christ's, then you are Abraham's offspring, heirs according to promise" (Gal. 3:29).

Abraham *and* Isaac went home. God did not love Abraham more because he obeyed, but Abraham knew and loved God more.

$\mathscr{P}$oints to $\mathscr{P}$onder

***Abraham acted on the basis of his knowledge of God.
Do you, or do you act on the basis of your feelings and fears?***

***How does the name Jehovah Jireh
strengthen and comfort you?***

***What are the Jesus sightings
you see in this chapter?***

Transformed by Prayer

All your works shall give thanks to you, O LORD,

and all your saints shall bless you!

They shall speak of the glory of your kingdom

and tell of your power,

to make known to the children of man your mighty deeds,

and the glorious splendor of your kingdom.

Your kingdom is an everlasting kingdom,

and your dominion endures throughout all generations.

(Ps. 145:10-13)

Home: Genesis 23

I want to love with a kindness that nurtures a hard heart to desire to be soft. God is the only one able to transform someone else's heart, but if I live a life submitted to Him, then His love will be reflected through me.[7]

Kara Tippetts

Genesis 22 pictures the magnificent mercy of God in providing a Substitutionary Sacrifice for sinners. It also personalizes the power of the gospel in the lives of the people in the narrative. We must be careful not to moralize, but it is appropriate to draw out lessons for faith and life *enfleshed* in these people. We will particularly look at Sarah, and we have ancillary Scriptures to guide us.

Sarah was chosen and protected by God. She was given faith to believe the impossible (Heb. 11:11). God tells those who pursue righteousness to "Look to ... Sarah who bore you" (Isa. 51:2), and Peter does that when he refers to her as an example of "the imperishable beauty of a gentle and quiet spirit, which in God's sight is very precious" (1 Pet. 3:4).

The question then is, did Sarah know what Abraham was going to do when he and Isaac left for Moriah? Because Scripture is silent, any conclusion is hypothetical, but I think she did. Even if Abraham did not tell her, she had lived with him for decades. A woman knows when her loved ones are troubled. I don't think Sarah thought this was just a camping trip. I wonder about their conversation through the night. How did she feel as she watched them walk away? I'm stunned that she did not chase them to offer an alternate plan. This would be any mother's most frightening hour, but it may be Sarah's finest hour. I wonder if this moment was in Peter's mind when he writes that "Sarah obeyed Abraham, calling him lord" (1 Pet.3: 6).

And what about Isaac? He is probably a teenager. Abraham is over a hundred years old. Do we really think the old man could tie the young guy onto the altar without his consent? We are not told about Sarah's mothering, but it is not hard to imagine how she loved her boy. It's not hard to imagine her telling him about the God who did the impossible to give him to her. Neither is it hard to imagine her hugging him that morning and whispering, "Remember, obey your dad, even if it seems frightening. You can trust him because he trusts God."

I think there is reason to believe Sarah is a transformed woman, so she reflects God's glorious grace into this highly emotional situation. Her life-giving heart sacrificially helps and inspires her people to trust and obey God.

We read about Sarah's laughter of unbelief (Gen. 18:12), but, like Eve, her reference point gradually changed from "I" to "God" and at the birth of Isaac she said, "God has made laughter for me; everyone who hears will laugh over me" (Gen. 21:6). I suspect her home was filled with happy, contagious laughter because she became a woman who "laughs at the time to come" (Prov. 31:25). She can laugh at the future because it does not frighten her. She is a holy, hopeful, heir of the grace of life. And when she welcomes Abraham and Isaac home there is love and laughter.

> Sarah lived 127 years; these were the years of the life of Sarah. And Sarah died ... and Abraham went in to mourn for Sarah and to weep for her. (23:1-2)

Abraham purchased property and "buried Sarah his wife in the cave of the field of Machpelah east of Mamre (that is, Hebron) in the land of Canaan" (Gen 23:19). This property was a token that one day the land would belong to the descendants of Abraham and Sarah. Sarah never owned a home on this earth, but because she was chosen by God *He* was her dwelling place.

> The eternal God is your dwelling place,
> and underneath are the everlasting arms ... (Deut. 33:27)

When God is our home, we are never homeless. We are always safe, so our presence can be a welcoming, happy home for others. The home of a life-giver can be a little glimpse of the happy home Jesus is preparing for us.

*P*oints to *P*onder

If you could have coffee with Sarah, what do you think she would tell you about God?

What would she tell you about seeing life in the context of the scope of the whole rather than in bits and pieces?

What would she tell you about the fork in the road?

Transformed by Prayer

How lovely is your dwelling place,

*O L*ORD *of hosts!*

My soul longs, yes, faints

*for the courts of the L*ORD*;*

my heart and flesh sing for joy

to the living God.

Even the sparrow finds a home,

and the swallow a nest for herself,

where she may lay her young,

*at your altars, O L*ORD *of hosts,*

my King and my God.

Blessed are those who dwell in your house, ever singing your praise! ... For a day in your courts is better

than a thousand elsewhere.

I would rather be a doorkeeper in the house of my God

than dwell in the tents of wickedness.

*O L*ORD *of hosts,*

blessed is the one who trusts in you!

(Ps. 84:1-4, 10, 12)

EIGHT

Mary's Son and Savior
Luke 1–2

ABBY'S STORY

Abby Golden is a recent Women's Ministry Graduate from the Moody Bible Institute. She lives in Chicago, Illinois.

At the tender age of five I felt unaccepted by other children and ignored by the adults in my church. I tried to earn their love and acceptance which led me to believe I had to earn God's love as well. Church did not feel like a safe place to me and I was moving down a dangerous path of hating God and the church.

Because of one woman, things changed dramatically when I was ten. A Christian family from outside of my church became a part of my life. The mother of this family quickly took on the role of being a spiritual mother to me. Through this relationship I learned that she loved me even when I made mistakes because that's how Jesus loves us. She taught me about integrity, loyalty, and hospitality and lovingly confronted me when I made wrong choices. Even as a teenager I could see the contrast between women who ignored me and this woman who loved me. I did not know the terms *life-taker* and *life-giver*, but I knew the reality. Interestingly, the Lord used both examples to plant within my heart a desire to make church a safe, nurturing, happy home for others. Eventually this desire became a passion to pursue a degree in women's ministry.

My experience and observations convince me that women are the heart-beat of the church. Women determine the atmosphere. And this can be positive or negative. I don't think the women in my church were mean. They were simply unaware and their indifference almost took the spiritual breath out of a little girl. But one woman made a difference, and now I get to disciple women and to tell them about our redemptive calling to be life-givers and about the power of our Savior to transform us from life-takers to life-givers. And I get to see the results in the relationships in our church family.

THINKING BIBLICALLY

A standard way of thinking about the whole picture of God's dealing with humanity begins with a good creation, spoiled by Adam's fall, redeemed by Christ's provision, and perfected in the consummation of Christ's rule over all things. This creation-fall-redemption-consummation perspective helps us map all the events of Scripture. All have a place in this great unfolding plan of "his-story".[1]

Bryan Chapell

Luke 1

²⁶In the sixth month the angel Gabriel was sent from God to a city of Galilee named Nazareth,

²⁷to a virgin betrothed to a man whose name was Joseph, of the house of David. And the virgin's name was Mary.

²⁸And he came to her and said, "Greetings, O favored one, the Lord is with you!"

²⁹But she was greatly troubled at the saying, and tried to discern what sort of greeting this might be.

³⁰And the angel said to her, "Do not be afraid, Mary, for you have found favor with God.

³¹And behold, you will conceive in your womb and bear a son, and you shall call his name Jesus.

³²He will be great and will be called the Son of the Most High. And the Lord God will give to him the throne of his father David,

³³and he will reign over the house of Jacob forever, and of his kingdom there will be no end."

³⁴And Mary said to the angel, "How will this be, since I am a virgin?"

³⁵And the angel answered her, "The Holy Spirit will come upon you, and the power of the Most High will overshadow you; therefore the child to be born will be called holy–the Son of God.

³⁶And behold, your relative Elizabeth in her old age has also conceived a son, and this is the sixth month with her who was called barren.

³⁷For nothing will be impossible with God."

- How does the angel define Mary in verse 28?
- What does the angel tell Mary about God in verse 28?
- Underline what you learn about Jesus.
- What emotion does the angel identify in verse 30?

The defining moment in redemptive history is announced with elegant simplicity. Surely a swirl of emotions spins in Mary's heart. The wonder of an angelic encounter. The apprehension of the unknown. Anxiety over how Joseph and others will receive the news. Confusion about how this is possible. The angel names the root of these emotions, warning Mary that the road before her divides between fear and faith.

The angel's greeting gives Mary the information she needs to choose the right road. *Favored* is the Greek word *charis*, which means grace. Mary is set apart by God as a recipient of His grace. "The Lord is with you" would likely remind her of the covenant promise: "I will be your God, you will be my people, I will dwell among you." (Gen. 17:7; Exod. 6:7; Deut. 29:12-13; Jer. 24:7; Zech. 8:8).

The miracle of the virgin birth will be accomplished by the power and protection of the Holy Spirit. Before Mary can react, she is reminded of Mother Sarah's legacy, which is now being experienced by Elizabeth: *Nothing is impossible with God.* It's interesting that the angel inserts the information about Elizabeth. Can it be that God wants Mary to experience the Titus 2 discipleship of an older woman training her for her mission?

Even though Mary has never known or seen a pregnant virgin, she chooses the way of faith: "Now faith is the assurance of things hoped for, the conviction of things not seen" (Heb. 11:1).

[38] *And Mary said, "Behold, I am the servant of the Lord; let it be to me according to your word." And the angel departed from her.*

- How does Mary define herself?
- To what authority does she submit?
- What will it mean for you to apply Mary's testimony to the relationships and situations in your life?

By identifying herself as God's servant, Mary declares her chief end: God's glory. She also declares her authority: God's word. Despite the tangle of emotions, Mary's singular purpose is servitude. The angel summons her, as Paul summons us, "by the mercies of God, to present your bodies as a living sacrifice, holy and acceptable to God, which is your spiritual worship" (Rom. 12:1). Her decision to surrender is based on the character of God and the nature of His promises. Trust and obedience are the overriding forces in her life. Mary's decisive response propels her down the road of transformation.

³⁹*In those days Mary arose and went with haste into the hill country, to a town in Judah,*

⁴⁰*and she entered the house of Zechariah and greeted Elizabeth.*

⁴¹*And when Elizabeth heard the greeting of Mary, the baby leaped in her womb. And Elizabeth was filled with the Holy Spirit,*

⁴²*and she exclaimed with a loud cry, "Blessed are you among women, and blessed is the fruit of your womb!*

⁴³*And why is this granted to me that the mother of my Lord should come to me?*

⁴⁴*For behold, when the sound of your greeting came to my ears, the baby in my womb leaped for joy.*

⁴⁵*And blessed is she who believed that there would be a fulfillment of what was spoken to her from the Lord."*

- Why do you think Mary hurried to Elizabeth's home?
- Is there an older woman you go to when you are at a divided road?

Elizabeth speaks of the baby in Mary's womb as "my Lord", putting the focus on *Him* and not *them*. She speaks life-giving words, and Mary sings.

⁴⁶*And Mary said, "My soul magnifies the Lord,*

⁴⁷*and my spirit rejoices in God my Savior,*

⁴⁸*for he has looked on the humble estate of his servant. For behold, from now on all generations will call me blessed;*

⁴⁹*for he who is mighty has done great things for me, and holy is his name.*

⁵⁰*And his mercy is for those who fear him from generation to generation.*

⁵¹*He has shown strength with his arm; he has scattered the proud in the thoughts of their hearts;*

⁵²*he has brought down the mighty from their thrones and exalted those of humble estate;*

⁵³*he has filled the hungry with good things, and the rich he has sent empty away.*

⁵⁴*He has helped his servant Israel, in remembrance of his mercy,*

⁵⁵*as he spoke to our fathers, to Abraham and to his offspring forever."*

⁵⁶*And Mary remained with her about three months and returned to her home.*

- Circle the words "He has".
- Underline the things Mary says God has done for her in Luke 1:48-49.
- How has God been merciful to humble, hungry, helpless people?
- What is the connection between Abraham and Sarah and Mary, and us?

Mary celebrates the God who said "I will" in the Old Testament as the God who "has" in her life. Mary's heart is melted by the mercy and majesty of God who transforms humble, hungry, helpless people into holy, hopeful heirs of the grace of life.

LIVING COVENANTALLY

For me, the Lord's Supper is always a powerful visual symbol. Maybe it's because we actually handle the bread and lift the wine to our lips. Yet as the plate of crackers is passed, we're ever so careful to ... aim for our cracker without touching any of the others. Our fastidious care, although tidy, also seems symbolic: we go to such extraordinary efforts to live our lives totally isolated from each other, even though we are one in Christ ...

I thought of that when my friend sitting next to me reached into the plate to get crackers for both of us. Then ... she lifted one piece to my mouth and then, the other piece to hers. I can't take communion myself ... I'm forced to depend on another Christian to handle my bread for me.

I'm glad about that. It makes me feel connected. Interdependent. One with others. It's a happy symbol of how closely I must live my life with fellow believers. I can't live my life alone and isolated.[2]

Joni Eareckson Tada

Elizabeth's Story: Luke 1:1-25

"... Elizabeth will bear you a son, and you shall call his name John ... And he will turn many of the children of Israel to the Lord their God, and he will go before him in the spirit and power of Elijah .... to make ready for the Lord a people prepared."

(Luke 1:13, 16-17)

The dawn of the New Testament begins with an old man and his barren wife.

In the days of Herod, king of Judea, there was a priest named Zechariah, of the division of Abijah. And he had a wife from the daughters of Aaron, and her name was Elizabeth. And they were both righteous before God, walking blamelessly in all the commandments and statutes of the Lord. But they had no child, because Elizabeth was barren, and both were advanced in years. (Luke 1:5-7)

Rome ruled, or so it seemed. This was a dark time in Israel's history. In addition to civil oppression, the old couple suffered the personal sorrow of barrenness; however, bitterness did not darken their souls. Behind the incredible commendation "they were both righteous before God, walking blamelessly" shines the sustaining grace and glory of God. By referencing Zechariah's and Elizabeth's link with the Old Testament, Luke skillfully places this narrative in the redemptive/historical context of God's plan and purpose.

Now while he was serving as priest before God ... there appeared to him an angel of the Lord standing on the right side of the altar of incense ... the angel said to him, "Do not be afraid, Zechariah, for your prayer has been heard and your wife Elizabeth will bear you a son, and you shall call his name John." (Luke 1:8, 11, 13)

What prayer had been heard? This probably refers to Zechariah's prayer at the altar for the redemption of Israel, for the coming of Messiah. This is a transformative prayer. For years as Zechariah and Elizabeth prayed for a son, they also prayed for a Savior. When it seemed the answer to the first prayer was "no" the second prayer continued. When our prevailing prayer is "Your kingdom come" every other prayer is subsumed to that, and our walk is increasingly blameless because we "consider that the sufferings of this present time are not worth comparing with the glory that is to be revealed to us" (Rom. 8:18).

> *After these days his wife Elizabeth conceived, and for five months she kept herself hidden, saying, "Thus the Lord has done for me in the days when* **he looked on me***, to take away my reproach among people."* (Luke 1:24-25)

Elizabeth's testimony proclaims the gospel. It seems likely that this "daughter of Aaron" was reflecting on the Aaronic blessing.

> *The* LORD *bless you and keep you;*
> *the* LORD *make his face to shine upon you and be gracious to you;*
> *the* LORD *lift up his countenance upon you and give you peace.*
> (Num. 6:24-26)

It is also likely that Hannah's prayer shaped Elizabeth's story.

> *... O* LORD *of hosts, if you will indeed* **look** *on the affliction of your servant and remember me and not forget your servant, but will give to your servant a son, then I will give him to the* LORD *all the days of his life ...* (1 Sam. 1:11)

He looked on me is the grateful testimony of daughters of Sarah. In Christ, He shines His face upon us and takes away the reproach and guilt of our sin. It must be noted – He can look *on* us because He looked *away* from His beloved Son as He bore our sin (Matt. 27:46). Now He looks on us with delight because He looks and sees Jesus.

What are your reactions to Elizabeth's testimony in Luke 1:25?

What does Elizabeth's story teach you about God?

Transformed by Prayer

Jesus said, "Pray then like this:

"Our Father in heaven,

hallowed be your name.

Your kingdom come,

your will be done,

on earth as it is in heaven.

Give us this day our daily bread,

and forgive us our debts,

as we also have forgiven our debtors.

And lead us not into temptation,

but deliver us from evil.

For yours is the kingdom and the power and the glory, forever. Amen"

(Matt. 6:9-13)

Mary's Song: Luke 1:46-55

Unbelief would have said, "Wait." Fear would have said, "Be silent." But faith could not wait and could not be silent! She must sing and sing she did most sweetly.[3]

Charles Haddon Spurgeon

After being in the safety of Elizabeth's presence, Mary sings the *Magnificat*, a song of praise that has blessed the church down through the ages. We must stop and ask: are the women in my life singing? Am I sharing the gospel, in the context of a loving relationship, so that their lives magnify the Lord?

Magnification can be like a microscope that makes small things appear bigger than they are. It can also be like a telescope that brings big things near. Mary's song brings the grandeur and glory of God near. Her "May it be as you have said" fuels her magnification of a magnificent God. Surrender and worship meet.

Mary's song shows that she knew the Old Testament. Perhaps Elizabeth was one of the people who taught her "from childhood ... the sacred writings, which are able to make you wise for salvation through faith in Christ Jesus" (2 Tim. 3:15). But Mary was not merely *informed*. This celebratory song erupts from a *transformed* heart. It follows the pattern of Psalms of Thanksgiving, beginning with expressions of gratitude and then telling the reason for the praise.

It is fascinating that Mary uses the phrase "he has looked on me" (Luke 1:48). It seems likely that Elizabeth shared her testimony with Mary, "Thus the Lord has done for me in the days when *he looked on me*, to take away my reproach among people" (Luke 1:25). And Mary repeats her spiritual mother's words.

There are striking parallels with Hannah's song of jubilation in 1 Samuel 2:1-10. Mary echoes Hannah's gratitude for the life-giving reversals brought about by the gospel (Luke 1:51-53; 1 Sam. 2:4-8). Hannah's legacy traveled through the centuries to the heart of Mary.

Mary refers to the helper ministry of God: "He has helped his servant Israel, in remembrance of his mercy, as he spoke to our fathers, to Abraham and to his offspring forever" (Luke 1:54-55).

Martyn Lloyd-Jones explains that the Greek word translated "help" means to "succor ... or, perhaps better still, to lift up. The people of Israel had been cast down ... he takes hold of them and helps them to stand upon their feet."[4]

Mary concludes by reaching back to Abraham, showing that she understands the scope of the redemption story. The promise of Genesis 12:3 that in Abraham "all the families of the earth shall be blessed" is being fulfilled.

Points to Ponder

How do some women make you feel safe in their presence?

How have you seen women "lift up" others?

How have you seen women tear others down?

How are you magnifying God, bringing His grandeur and glory near, in the routines of your life?

How are you giving a legacy of joyful praise to women and girls in your life?

Transformed by Prayer

Jesus' prayer for you

"Father, the hour has come; glorify your Son that the Son may glorify you, since you have given him authority over all flesh, to give eternal life to all whom you have given him ... I am not praying for the world but for those whom you have given me, for they are yours. All mine are yours, and yours are mine, and I am glorified in them ... Holy Father, keep them in your name, which you have given me, that they may be one, even as we are one."

(John 17:1-2, 9-11)

Pierced: Luke 2:22-38

Jesus said: "Love your enemies, do good to those who hate you, bless those who curse you, pray for those who abuse you."
(Luke 6:27-28)

In obedience to the Law of Moses, Mary and Joseph take Jesus to the temple to "present Him to the Lord" (Luke 2:22). Simeon, led by the Holy Spirit, approaches them, takes the baby in his arms, prophetically points to the glory and scope of the gospel for Gentiles as well as Jews, and then speaks shocking words to Mary:

Behold, this child is appointed for the fall and rising of many in Israel, and for a sign that is opposed (and a sword will pierce through your own soul also), so that thoughts from many hearts may be revealed. (Luke 2:34-35)

Remember, Mary knew God's Word. Did that Word vibrate through her whole being? Did she glimpse the mission of her baby?

For dogs encompass me;
a company of evildoers encircles me;
*they have **pierced** my hands and feet—*
I can count all my bones—
they stare and gloat over me;
they divide my garments among them,
and for my clothing they cast lots.
But you, O LORD, do not be far off!
O you my help, come quickly to my aid! (Ps. 22:16-19)

*And I will pour out on the house of David and the inhabitants of Jerusalem a spirit of grace and pleas for mercy, so that, when they look on me, on him whom they have **pierced**, they shall mourn for him, as one mourns for an only child, and weep bitterly over him, as one weeps over a firstborn.* (Zech. 12:10)

*But one of the soldiers **pierced** his side with a spear ... For these things took place that the Scripture might be fulfilled: ... "They will look on him whom they have pierced."* (John 19:34, 36, 37)

The Greek word used for sword depicts a large sword, much like the one Goliath used. The action of this sword would be characterized by a constant, ongoing piercing. As Mary staggers under the weight of these words, God sends an eighty-four year old widow to her side.

> And there was a prophetess, Anna, the daughter of Phanuel, of the tribe of Asher. She was advanced in years, having lived with her husband seven years from when she was a virgin, and then as a widow until she was eighty-four. She did not depart from the temple, worshiping with fasting and prayer night and day. And coming up at that very hour she began to give thanks to God and to speak of him to all who were waiting for the redemption of Jerusalem. (Luke 2:36-38)

This holy woman who hopes in God speaks life-giving words to the young woman with a sword in her soul. She speaks words of gratitude for the Redeemer and the redemption He would accomplish. We, too, can be life-givers to women with a sword in their soul, not by denying the pain of the sword, but by helping them see it in the context of the redemption planned in eternity past and accomplished by Mary's Son. He suffered the sword of judgment so that the swords that pierce our souls will not be used to punish us but to carve us into His likeness.

Daughters of Sarah are not spared the swords. Some swords in our souls are the result of our own sin. Some are because of the sin of others against us. And some are due to our providential circumstances such as illness or the death of a loved one. We all need women who teach us that pain and peace can co-exist in our hearts because Jesus brought peace on earth. We need Elizabeths and Annas to remind us that because of redemption, our sins which pierced Jesus are forgiven, so we are freed to be forgivers even to those who thrust a sword into our soul. We need women to tell us to look beyond the sword to the consummation.

> Behold, he is coming with the clouds, and every eye will see him, even those who **pierced** him ...(Rev. 1:7)

Points to Ponder

When have you experienced a sword piercing your soul?

What are some ways women were life-givers to you?

What are your thoughts about forgiving those who thrust a sword into our soul?

What difference does it make to see the sword in the context of redemption?

Transformed by Prayer

Jesus' prayer for you

"I have given them your word, and the world has hated them because they are not of the world, just as I am not of the world. I do not ask that you take them out of the world, but that you keep them from the evil one. They are not of the world, just as I am not of the world. Sanctify them in the truth; your word is truth."
(John 17:14-17)

Glory Breaks Through: John 1–2:12

Now to him who is able to keep you from stumbling and to present you blameless before the presence of his glory with great joy, to the only God, our Savior, through Jesus Christ our Lord, be glory, majesty, dominion, and authority, before all time and now and forever. Amen.

(Jude 24-25)

The soaring beauty of Jude's and John's language captivates the imagination, compels the heart, and transforms the life.

In the beginning was the Word, and the Word was with God, and the Word was God. He was in the beginning with God. All things were made through him, and without him was not anything made that was made ... And the Word became flesh and dwelt among us, and we have seen his glory, glory as of the only Son from the Father, full of grace and truth. (John 1:1-3, 14)

The Word, the second Person of the Trinity, spoke creation into existence. And then, in the fullness of time, the Word became flesh. In His fleshness, He brought glory from heaven to this dark and fallen world.

I want to wrap my head and heart around this. The love and mercy and grace and wonder of it are endless. It's eternal. I want to be so wrapped up *in* that glory, *in Christ*, that it overtakes me. It transforms me. It shines through me. The more I see, the more I want to see what glory in the flesh looks like, so I have been pondering some specific events when glory broke through.

On the third day there was a wedding at Cana in Galilee, and the mother of Jesus was there. (John 2:1)

The third day ... is this whispering to us that it would be on the third day our heavenly Bridegroom would come triumphantly from the grave, conquering sin and death? Is it reminding us that it is Resurrection Power that will enable us to reflect glory?

Jesus also was invited to the wedding with his disciples. When the wine ran out, the mother of Jesus said to him, "They have no wine." And Jesus said to her, "Woman, what does this have to do with me? My hour has not yet come." His mother said to the servants, **"Do whatever he tells you."** *(John 2:2-5)*

Mary has learned that obedience is a path to becoming a life-giver, so with five simple words she spiritually mothers us to trust and obey Him even when, *especially when*, we have nothing left.

Now there were six stone water jars there for the Jewish rites of purification, each holding twenty or thirty gallons. Jesus said to the servants, "Fill the jars with water." And they filled them up to the brim. And he said to them, "Now draw some out and take it to the master of the feast." So they took it. When the master of the feast tasted the water now become wine, and did not know where it came from (though the servants who had drawn the water knew), the master of the feast called the bridegroom and said to him, "Everyone serves the good wine first, and when people have drunk freely, then the poor wine. But you have kept the good wine until now." This, the first of his signs, Jesus did at Cana in Galilee, and manifested his glory. And his disciples believed in him. (John 2:6-11)

Jesus takes empty vessels, purifies us, and fills us with living water (John 4:10; 7:38; Rev. 7:17). By His power sinful, empty, dead people are transformed into people filled with abundant life (John 10:10). And soon, without us even being aware of it, this life spills out on dry, thirsty people and places. Glory breaks through as we begin to manifest His goodness, mercy, grace, love, faithfulness, and forgiveness (Exod. 4:6-7). Amazing, transforming, life-giving grace!

Points to Ponder

When have you seen glory break through — God's goodness in yourself or another?

Celebrate and affirm it. Tell people when you see God's goodness in them.

Transformed by Prayer

Jesus' prayer for you

"I do not ask for these only, but also for those who will believe in me through their word, that they may all be one, just as you, Father, are in me, and I in you, that they also may be in us, so that the world may believe that you have sent me. The glory that you have given me I have given to them, that they may be one even as we are one, I in them and you in me, that they may become perfectly one, so that the world may know that you sent me and loved them even as you loved me."

(John 17:20-23)

God with us: Luke 2:1-20

All this took place to fulfill what the Lord had spoken by the prophet: "Behold, the virgin shall conceive and bear a son, and they shall call his name Immanuel" (which means, God with us).
(Matt. 1:22-23; Isa, 7:14)

When Isaiah's prophecy was fulfilled, and God came to be with us, He provided the young virgin with spiritual mothers, one at a time of rejoicing, another at a time of weeping.

Elizabeth's home was a safe place for Mary. These women were gospel friends with gospel commonalities. They were recipients of God's grace and favor. They shared humanly impossible pregnancies. They had waited expectantly for the Messiah. They faced unknown futures with the faith that God is with us.

Elizabeth shared the gospel and her life with young Mary. She spoke Spirit-led, life-giving words of blessing, hope, affirmation and instruction to the younger woman, and Mary returned home prepared for what followed — a trip to Bethlehem, a stable, angels, shepherds, and a baby. The baby holy women before her hoped in.

Mary treasured up all these things, pondering them in her heart.
(Luke 2:19)

At a time of weeping, Anna made the temple a safe place for Mary. Anna's name means beautiful grace. This holy, hopeful widow lived with a holy expectancy that God would come, and when He did she encouraged Mary to see the redemptive beauty of the painful sword that would pierce her soul.

Women who treasure and ponder the transforming truth that God is with us have "the imperishable beauty of a gentle and quiet spirit, which in God's sight is very precious (1 Pet. 3:4). They "do good" to the people God puts in their lives and "do not fear anything that is frightening" (1 Pet. 3:6) because they "entrust their souls to a faithful Creator" (1 Pet. 4:19).

Elizabeth and Anna prepared Mary for the frightening places the road of faith would take her.

> *Now when they [the wise men] had departed, behold, an angel*
> *of the Lord appeared to Joseph in a dream and said, "Rise, take*
> *the child and his mother, and flee to Egypt, and remain there*
> *until I tell you, for Herod is about to search for the child, to*
> *destroy him." And he rose and took the child and his mother by*
> *night and departed to Egypt and remained there until the death*
> *of Herod. This was to fulfill what the Lord had spoken by the*
> *prophet, "Out of Egypt I called my son." (Matt. 2:13-15)*

Mary, Joseph, and Jesus are elect exiles. Mary and Joseph grew
up celebrating the Passover, and now they are told to go to
Egypt, the setting for the first Passover and God's deliverance.
Mary's "May it be to me as you have said" decision led her to
the foot of a cross where she would watch her son become our
Passover Lamb. Perhaps she remembered the Egypt experience
and was comforted that neither Pharaoh nor Herod nor Pontus
Pilate could extinguish God's ordained deliverers.

> *When Jesus saw his mother and the disciple whom he loved*
> *standing nearby, he said to his mother, "Woman, behold, your*
> *son!" Then he said to the disciple, "Behold, your mother!" And*
> *from that hour the disciple took her to his own home.*
> (John 19:26-27)

Mary was called to be the life-giver to the Ultimate Life-Giver. At
this place of death, His tender words extend life-giving love to
her. Did she ponder the promise that nothing is impossible for
God and that He brings life from death? Jesus, the seed of her
first mother Eve, will crush Satan's head. Jesus, the Offspring
of her spiritual mother Sarah, is the One through whom all the
nations will be blessed. Jesus is not only Mary's son; He is her
Savior.

Pondering the treasures in her heart prepared Mary to
follow her Savior to the cross, to watch His ascension into
heaven, to gather in the upper room with those who were
"devoting themselves to prayer" as they waited for the Holy
Spirit (Acts 1:9-14), and to join the great host of "women who
announce the news" (Ps. 68:11) as they share their transforming
treasure with others.

$\mathscr{P}$oints to $\mathscr{P}$onder

Do you treasure and ponder the gospel?

Is your life characterized by a holy expectancy?

Ponder the magnitude of "God with us", God with me. What difference does this make in your life?

God provided spiritual mothers for Mary at a time of rejoicing and a time of weeping.

Are we doing the same for women in our covenant community?

What have you learned from Eve, Sarah, and Mary that will help you when you stand at a birfurcated road?

What themes have you seen woven through this book?

Transformed by Prayer

Jesus' prayer for you

"Father, I desire that they also, whom you have given me, may be with me where I am, to see my glory that you have given me because you loved me before the foundation of the world. O righteous Father, even though the world does not know you, I know you, and these know that you have sent me. I made known to them your name, and I will continue to make it known, that the love with which you have loved me may be in them, and I in them."

(John 17:24-26)

EPILOGUE

Dear Reader-friend,

It's done! We actually finished by the deadline. And you have finished reading it.

The process of writing this book drew us closer to our Savior and to one another. We have known sweet fellowship with Him and with each other as we have prayed that the words would be "from Him and through Him and to Him" and for His glory. The process also drew our hearts to you as we prayed for those who will read it. Wednesday will be our day to continue praying for you. Please join us and pray for women who have read, are reading, and will read this book, but above all let's pray that women will read The Book.

Let's read The Book because we do "not live by bread alone, but man lives by every word that comes from the mouth of the LORD" (Deut. 8:3) and God promises that His Word "shall not return to me empty, but it shall accomplish that which I purpose, and shall succeed in the thing for which I sent it" (Isa. 55:11).

Read The Book because our Father tells us that we will "shine as lights in the world" by "holding fast to the word of life" (Phil. 2:16), so "Let the word of Christ dwell in you richly" (Col. 3:16) because "it is living and active, sharper than any two-edged sword, piercing to the division of soul and of spirit, of joints and of marrow, and discerning the thoughts and intentions of the heart" (Heb. 4:12).

Never forget, His Word is "no empty word for you, but your very life, and by this word you shall live" (Deut. 32:47).

We are deeply grateful for the women who shared their transforming stories. We encourage you to write your own transforming story. Think about Eve, Sarah, and Mary. Most of all ... think about our Triune God and His transforming love for us. Then write your story.

I thank my God in all my remembrance of you, always in every prayer of mine for you all making my prayer with joy, because of your partnership in the gospel from the first day until now. And I am sure of this, that he who began a good work in you will bring it to completion at the day of Jesus Christ. It is right for me to feel this way about you all, because I hold you in my heart, for you are all partakers with me of grace, both in my imprisonment and in the defense and confirmation of the gospel. For God is my witness, how I yearn for you all with the affection of Christ Jesus. And it is my prayer that your love may abound more and more, with knowledge and all discernment, so that you may approve what is excellent, and so be pure and blameless for the day of Christ, filled with the fruit of righteousness that comes through Jesus Christ, to the glory and praise of God.

Philippians 1:3-11

Karen & Susan

ENDNOTES

Chapter 1

1. *Gospel Transformation Bible, Introduction to the ESV Gospel Transformation Bible* (Wheaton, IL: Crossway, 2015), vii.

2. *Gospel Transformation Bible, Introduction to 1 Peter*, Ibid, 1685.

3. *Westminster Shorter Catechism* (Atlanta, GA.: Presbyterian Church in America Committee for Christian Education & Publications, 1990), 3.

4. *Westminster Larger Catechism* (Atlanta, GA.: Presbyterian Church in America Committee for Christian Education & Publications, 1990), 4.

5. John MacArthur, *The MacArthur New Testament Commentary 1 Peter* (Chicago, IL.: Moody Publishers, 2004), 27.

6. *Westminster Confession of Faith*, VII, Of God's Covenant with Man (Atlanta, GA.: Presbyterian Church in America Committee for Christian Education & Publications, 1990), 24.

Chapter 2

1. *Westminster Confession of Faith*, Chapter 1. 9, Of the Holy Scripture, Ibid., 3.

2. Philip Graham Ryken, editor, *The Communion of Saints* (Phillipsburg, N.J.: P & R Publishing, 2001), 9.

3. James Montgomery Boice, *The Gospel of John, Vol. 4* (Grand Rapids, MI.: Baker Books, 1999), 1248.

4. C. S. Lewis, *Mere Christianity* (New York: Collier Books, 1952), 140.

5. Nikolaus Ludwig von Zinzendorf, *Jesus, Thy Blood and Righteousness*, 1739, Tr. By John Wesley, 1740 (Atlanta, GA.: Great Commission Publications, 1990) 520.

6. W. E. Vine, *An Expository Dictionary of New Testament Words, Vol 3* (Old Tappan, N.J.: Fleming Revell, 1966), 55-56.

7. Timothy Keller, *The Freedom of Self-Forgetfulness* (Chorley, England, 10 Publishing, 2012) ebook 267.

8. W. E. Vine, *An Expository Dictionary of New Testament Words*, Ibid, 242.

9. *Westminster Confession of Faith*, Chap. XXVL, Of the Communion of the Saints (Atlanta, GA.: Committee for Christian Education & Publications, 1990), 85.

Chapter 3

1. David White, "*On the Road: Facing the Hard Questions*". Harvest USA magazine, Spring 2015.

2. Edmund P. Clowney, *The Unfolding Mystery–Discovering Christ in the Old Testament* (Phillipsburg, N.J.: P & R Publishing, 1988) 9, 11.

3. Michael Horton, *God of Promise* (Grand Rapids, MI.: Baker Publishing Group, 2007), 10

4. Ligon Duncan and Susan Hunt, *Women's Ministry in the Local Church* (Wheaton, IL.: Crossway Books, 2006), 32-33.

5. *Westminster Shorter Catechism* (Atlanta, GA.: Presbyterian Church in America Committee for Christian Education & Publications, 1990), 5.

6. Wayne Grudem, *Evangelical Feminism & Biblical Truth* (Sisters, OR.:, Multnomah Publishers, 2004) 48.

Chapter 4

1. Noel Piper, *Faithful Women & Their Extraordinary God* (Wheaton, IL.:, Crossway Books, 2005), 158-160.

2. *Gospel Transformation Bible*, Ibid., 9.

3. Susan Hunt & Barbara Thompson, *The Legacy of Biblical Womanhood* (Wheaton, IL.: Crossway Books, 2003), 111.

4. Michael Card, *A Sacred Sorrow* (Colorado Springs, CO.:, NavPress, 2005), 15.

5. Brian Roemmele, "The History of the "i" prefix in Apple Products Names," *Quora* (August 2, 2011. Web. February 23, 2016).

6. *Westminster Shorter Catechism* (Atlanta, GA.: Presbyterian Church in America Committee for Christian Education & Publications, 1990), 13.

7. James Montgomery Boice, *Genesis Volume 1* (Grand Rapids, MI.: Baker Books, 1982), 266.

8. Augustus Toplady, *Rock of Ages, Cleft for Me*, Trinity Hymnal (Atlanta, GA,: Great Commission Publications, 1990) 499.

9. Ann Voskamp, *Women's Devotional Bible*, My Soul Thirsts for You (Wheaton, IL.: Crossway, 2014), 660.

Endnotes

10. John Sammis, *Trust and Obey*, Trinity Hymnal (Atlanta, GA.: Great Commission Publications, 1990), 672.

Chapter 5

1. Bruce Waltke, *Genesis: A Commentary with the New International Version* (Grand Rapids, IL.: Zondervan, 2001) 205.

2. Walter Brueggemann, *Genesis, Interpretation: A Biblical Commentary for Teaching and Preaching.* First Edition (Louisville, KY.: Westminster John Knox Press, 2010) 118-119.

3. Charles Haddon Spurgeon, *The Treasury of the Bible, NT, Vol. 2* (Grand Rapids, MI.: Zondervan, 1962) 611.

4. Jen Wilkin, *Women of the Word: How to Study the Bible with Both Our Hearts and Our Minds* (Wheaton, IL.: Crossway Books, 2014) 26.

5. J. I. Packer, *Knowing God* (Downers Grove, IL.: InterVarsity Press, 1973), 33-34.

6. James Boice, *Genesis Volume 2* (Grand Rapids, MI.: Baker Books, 1985), 458-459.

Chapter 6

1. James Boice, *Genesis Volume 2* (Grand Rapids, MI.: Baker Books, 1985), 539.

2. John Calvin, *Institutes of the Christian Religion, Volume 1* (Philadelphia, PA.: The Westminster Press), 726.

3. James Boice, Ibid., 540.

4. Martin Luther, *What Luther Says: An Anthology*, comp. Ewald m. Plass, 2 vols. (St. Louis: Concordia, 1959), 2:702-4, 715 (cited in James Boice, Ibid., 540).

5. *Westminster Shorter Catechism Q. 33* (Atlanta, GA.: Presbyterian Church in America Committee for Christian Education & Publications, 1990), 12.

6. J. V. Fesko, *What is Justification by Faith Alone?* (Phillipsburg, N.J.: 2008), 13-14.

7. *Westminster Shorter Catechism Q. 35* (Atlanta, GA.: Presbyterian Church in America Committee for Christian Education & Publications, 1990), 13.

8. Ibid, Q. 37, 13.

9. Nancy Guthrie, *The Promised One, Seeing Jesus in Genesis* (Wheaton, IL.: Crossway, 2011), 165.

10. Tim Keller, *Galatians, Paul's Letter to the Galatians*, Leader's Guide (New York, Redeemer Presbyterian Church, 2003), 2.

11. Kevin DeYoung, "The Protestant debate over justification: Here I stand," *The Christian Science Monitor*, Nov. 30, 2009. http://www.csmonitor.com/Commentary/Opinion/2009/1130/p09s03-coop.html., accessed October 22, 2015.

12. Thomas Watson, *A Body of Divinity* (London: Banner of Truth, 1970), 226 (cited in James Boice, Ibid., 540).

Chapter 7

1. Bryan Jerrery Leech, *We Are God's People, Trinity Hymnal* (Atlanta, GA.: Great Commission Publications, 1990), 355.

2. Susannah Spurgeon, *Morning Devotions, Free Grace and Dying Love* (Edinburgh, UK.: The Banner of Truth Trust, 2006), 57.

3. Elisabeth Elliot, *A Lamp Unto my Feet* (Ventura, CA.: Regal Books, 1985), 29.

4. Joni Eareckson Tada, *Holiness in Hidden Places* (Nashville, TN.: Thomas Nelson, 1999), 108.

5. *Spirit of the Reformation Study Bible* (Grand Rapids, MI.: Zondervan, 2003) 46.

6. Elizabeth Prentiss, *More Love to Thee, O Christ*, Trinity Hymnal (Atlanta, GA.: Great Commission Publications, 1990), 649.

7. Kara Tippets, *Big Love, The Practice of loving beyond your limits*, ebook.

Chapter 8

1. *Gospel Transformation Bible*, Introduction, Ibid., vii.

2. Joni Eareckson Tada, *Holiness in Hidden Places* (Nashville, TN.: Thomas Nelson, Inc., 1999) 38.

3. Charles H. Spurgeon, Spurgeon's Sermons Volume 51, Mary's Magnificat, 1905, Grand Rapids, Christian Classics Ethereal. http//www.ccel.org/ccel/spurgeon/sermons51. xxvi.html.

4. Martyn Lloyd-Jones, excerpted from *My Soul Magnifies the Lord: Meditations on the Meaning of Christmas* by Martyn Lloyd-Jones. Copyright 1998 by Elizabeth Catherwood and Ann Lockwood. Quoted in *Come, Thou Long-Expected Jesus*, Nancy Guthrie (Wheaton, IL.: Crossway, 2008) 44.

Also available
from
Christian Focus Publications

THE

ENVY

OF *Eve*

FINDING CONTENTMENT IN
A COVETOUS WORLD

MELISSA B. KRUGER

ISBN 978-1-84550-775-6

The Envy of Eve
Finding Contentment in a Covetous World

MELISSA B. KRUGER

This book guides readers to understand how desires grow into covetousness and what happens when this sin takes power in our hearts. Covetousness chokes out the fruit of the Spirit in our lives, allowing discontentment to bloom. The key to overcoming is to get to the root of our problem: unbelief-a mistrust of God's sovereignty and goodness. An ideal resource for deeper study or group discussion.

With empathy and grounded biblical insight, Melissa Kruger shows us the path to abiding joy amidst life's varied 'ups' and 'downs'.

Lydia Brownback
Author of *Contentment*, Wheaton, Illinois

In an age and culture where we all tend to have an overdeveloped sense of entitlement, this book makes a brilliant diagnosis that goes right to the heart of the problem.

Ann Benton
Author and family conference speaker, Guildford, England

With I've-been-there understanding and been-in-the-Word insight, Melissa B. Kruger helps us to look beneath the surface of our discontent, exposing our covetous hearts to the healing light of God's Word.

Nancy Guthrie
Author of *Seeing Jesus in the Old Testament Bible Study Series*

Melissa B. Kruger serves as Women's Ministry Coordinator at Uptown Church in Charlotte, North Carolina and is a speaker at various Christian conferences across the United States. Her husband, Michael J. Kruger, is the president of Reformed Theological Seminary in Charlotte.

Christian Focus Publications

Our mission statement –

STAYING FAITHFUL
In dependence upon God we seek to impact the world through literature faithful to His infallible Word, the Bible. Our aim is to ensure that the Lord Jesus Christ is presented as the only hope to obtain forgiveness of sin, live a useful life and look forward to heaven with Him.

Our books are published in four imprints:

CHRISTIAN
FOCUS

Popular works including biographies, commentaries, basic doctrine and Christian living.

CHRISTIAN
HERITAGE

Books representing some of the best material from the rich heritage of the church.

MENTOR

Books written at a level suitable for Bible College and seminary students, pastors, and other serious readers. The imprint includes commentaries, doctrinal studies, examination of current issues and church history.

CF4•K

Children's books for quality Bible teaching and for all age groups: Sunday school curriculum, puzzle and activity books; personal and family devotional titles, biographies and inspirational stories – Because you are never too young to know Jesus!

Christian Focus Publications Ltd,
Geanies House, Fearn, Ross-shire,
IV20 1TW, Scotland, United Kingdom.
www.christianfocus.com